ALSO BY JAMES GALVIN

Imaginary Timber
God's Mistress
Elements

THE MEADOW

James Galvin

A Holt Paperback

Henry Holt and Company

New York

Holt Paperbacks
Henry Holt and Company, LLC
Publishers since 1866
175 Fifth Avenue
New York, New York 10010
www.henryholt.com

Library of Congress Cataloging-in-Publication Data
The meadow / by James Galvin.
p. cm.
ISBN-13: 978-0-8050-2703-7
ISBN-10: 0-8050-2703-3
I. Title.
PS3557.A444M43   1992   91-34277
813'.54—dc20   CIP

Henry Holt books are available for special promotions and
premiums. For details contact: Director Special Markets.

Originally published in hardcover in 1992 by
Henry Holt and Company

First Holt Paperbacks Edition 1993

Designed by Claire N. Vaccaro

Printed in the United States of America

D 40 39 38

Robert Duncan's poem (page vii) is from his collection
The Opening of the Field. Copyright © 1960 by Robert Duncan.
Reprinted by permission of New Direcions Publishing Corporation.

Acknowledgments

I wrote this book for Emily.

Thanks to Allan Gurganus, William Kittredge, Richard Kenney, Jorie Graham, William Strachan, Abigail Thomas, and Beverly Pepper for their help and encouragement. Special thanks to Curtis Bill Pepper for talking it out of me to begin with.

Thanks also to the John Simon Guggenheim Foundation for a grant which helped enormously in the writing of this book.

The text on page 131 first appeared in the *Coe Review* under the title, "Small Countries."

OFTEN I AM PERMITTED TO RETURN
TO A MEADOW

as if it were a scene made-up by the mind,
that is not mine, but is a made place,

that is mine, it is so near to the heart,
an eternal pasture folded in all thought
so that there is a hall therein

that is a made place, created by light
wherefrom the shadows that are forms fall.

Wherefrom fall all architectures I am
I say are likenesses of the First Beloved
whose flowers are flames lit to the Lady.

She it is Queen Under The Hill
whose hosts are a disturbance of words within words
that is a field folded.

It is only a dream of the grass blowing
east against the source of the sun
in an hour before the sun's going down

whose secret we see in a children's game
of ring a round of roses told.

Often I am permitted to return to a meadow
as if it were a given property of the mind
that certain bounds hold against chaos,

that is a place of first permission,
everlasting omen of what is.

—Robert Duncan

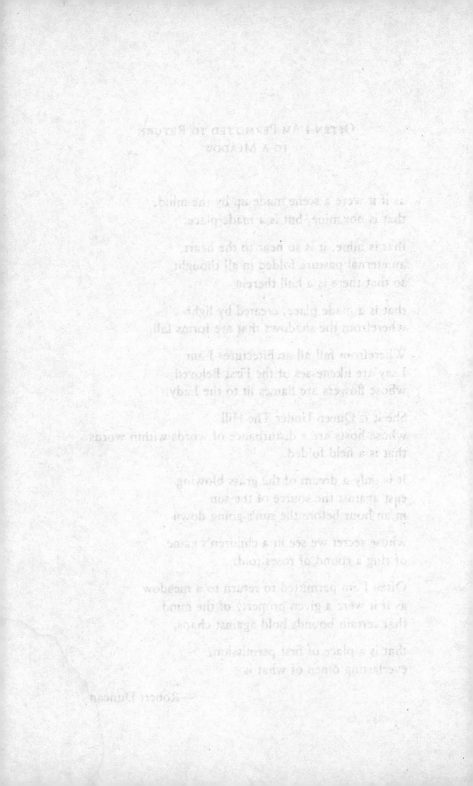

I.

The real world goes like this: The Neversummer Mountains like a jumble of broken glass. Snowfields weep slowly down. Chambers Lake, ringed by trees, gratefully catches the drip in its tin cup, and gives the mountains their own reflection in return. This is the real world, indifferent, unburdened.

Two rivers flow from opposite ends of Chambers Lake, like two ends of yarn being pulled off a spool at the same time. The Laramie River flows through its own valley, through its own town, then into the North Platte. From the opposing end of the lake the Cache la Poudre gouges into a steep canyon down to the South Platte River. At North Platte, Nebraska, the two forks of the Platte conjoin and the separate, long-traveled waters of Chambers Lake remarry.

The real world goes like this: Coming down from the high lake, timbered ridges in slow green waves suddenly stop and bunch up like patiently disappointed refugees, waiting for permission to start walking out across the open prairie toward Nebraska, where the waters come together and form an enormous inland island, large parts of three large states surrounded by water. The island never heard of states; the real world is the island.

There is an island on the island which is a meadow, offered up among the ridges, wearing a necklace of waterways, concentrically nested inside the darker green of pines, and then the gray-green of sage and the yellow-green of prairie grass.

The story of the meadow is a litany of loosely patterned weather, a chronicle of circular succession. Indians hunted here in summer, but they never wintered here, as far as we can tell, not on purpose. It's the highest cultivated ground

3

in this spur of the Medicine Bow, no other level terrain in sight. There have been four names on the deed to it, starting just a hundred years back.

The history of the meadow goes like this: No one owns it, no one ever will. The people, all ghosts now, were ghosts even then; they drifted through, drifted away, thinking they were not moving. They learned the recitations of seasons and the repetitive work that seasons require.

Only one of them succeeded in making a life here, for almost fifty years. He weathered. Before a backdrop of natural beauty, he lived a life from which everything was taken but a place. He lived so close to the real world it almost let him in.

By the end he had nothing, as if loss were a fire in which he was purified again and again, until he wasn't a ghost anymore.

The way people watch television while they eat—looking up to the TV and down to take a bite and back up—that's how Lyle watches the meadow out the south window while he eats his breakfast. He's hooked on the plot, doesn't want to miss anything. He looks out over the rim of his cup as he sips.

The meadow is under two feet of snow, which looks gray but not dirty in this light. Leafless willow branches make an orange streak down the middle. Each year the snow tries to memorize, blindly, the landscape, as if it were the landscape that was going to melt in spring.

The wind has cleared a couple of the knobs above the meadow, and the silver-gray sage throbs out. Above that stands the front line of timber, where the trees begin, or end, depending, still dead black though the sky has brightened behind it, a willing blue. Nothing is moving across the meadow this morning.

Yesterday sixteen elk streaked across the hillside above the meadow. Lyle could easily imagine what they had done to the fence where it runs under deep drifts on the east side. They walked through it, not even feeling the barbs through their winter coats. They dragged broken wire through the woods, strewing it like tinsel. He'd find the pieces in the spring like tendrils of steel briar growing along the ground. It doesn't make him angry anymore, as it did in the early years. He figures the elk have been crossing that section of timber to forage on the north side of Bull Mountain for a lot longer than there has been anyone here to build fence and get pissed off every time the elk tear it up. Now he splices the fence with baling wire, which is lighter, so it will break easier and always in the same place and not get dragged so much or pull out posts.

The first light hits the meadow and the kitchen window, and it's like Christmas lights going on. The trees go from black to loden green. The snow turns a mild electric blue and sparks.

A white crown sparrow lights on a small juniper branch that bends down and springs back up. Lyle says, "What kept you?" The sparrow hops onto the windowsill as a chickadee lights and begins bouncing up and down on the juniper branch just left by the other. "And you, you cheerful little sonofabitch, you don't waste no time either, do you?"

Lyle slowly straightens his stiff joints as he gets out of the chair and shuffles (his shoes are still untied) over to the wood stove. He picks up the plate with the extra pancake, carries it back to the table, and sits down. He cranks the window open about an inch—not enough for the birds to come in and kill themselves trying to get out—pinches off some warm pancake and crumbles it onto the outside sill. "Little beggars."

When the day's first visitors have finished their crumbs and flown, Lyle picks up a two-month-old newspaper Ed Wilkes brought and begins to read, but he is soon interrupted by a tiny beak tapping on the glass. This one is a junco, and then the chickadee is back, bouncing from branch to branch chirping. Lyle gives them some crumbs. Addressing the chickadee, "I don't know what you're so goddamn happy about all the time."

There's a racket of chirps and squawks by the front door. Lyle unbends out of the chair again, takes another pinch of flapjack to the door, and steps outside on the stoop. The screeching squawk is a Stellar's jay, who flees the wire he's perched on as soon as the door opens. He's had enough stones and snowballs pitched at him to know. To the little row of sparrows that has returned to the perch Lyle says, "That hatchet-head won't bother you now." All at once they fly down and light on his uplifted palm. They peck off pieces

6

of cake and flee back to the wire like greedy children waiting another turn. When the pancake is gone Lyle goes back inside to wash the dishes.

Once, coming back from town, I saw Lyle's truck parked at the Wooden Shoe. I stopped to say hello. Lyle was building a new garden fence, and as I approached, he held up his hand, a signal not to come closer. Then he leaned his shovel against the post he was setting and walked slowly across the garden to where a barn swallow was perched on a rail. Lyle took off his glove, and with the back of his huge index finger, touched the swallow gently under its throat, then ran his finger down once, gently, over its breast. Then he put his glove back on and walked away, and the bird took to the air again.

Lyle said, "Up close them swallows are the funniest damned looking things you ever saw. They fly like angels and then up close they look like little clowns. The damndest thing."

Lyle's thinning hair is the color of last year's grass next spring, fresh from under the long snow. He cuts it himself, so it's always nebulous on top and hacked away in patches above the back of his neck, which is red with chain link creases.

He would be almost homely if he didn't look so bright: long in the chin and nose, wide of mouth, eyes such a cutting pale blue that when he looks at you, he makes you think of whatever it is you are ashamed of. It's like he can smell your soul's feet.

I've never seen a stranger meet him who could return his stare. Not that he's trying something. He's just looking at you. I've known Lyle since I was two years old. There's nothing he doesn't know about me. That's the only reason I can look him in the eye.

Lyle is sixty-three. When he sits in a straight-backed chair he kind of folds himself down, like a folded union suit—the terrible posture of someone who is usually exhausted before they allow themselves to sit—legs crossed, hands in lap, almost liquid shoulders.

When he smiles at a joke you can see a lot of gold behind his teeth. And his eyes flare in their far blue.

Here's the first dream: Lyle is still Lyle, still driving the '59 Studebaker that sounds more like it runs on an electric motor than a gasoline one it's tuned so fine, but you can tell it's a dream when he drives it into Denver: the kind of detail that lets the dreamer know he's dreaming even as he dreams.

The dreamer, outside this dream, has only seen Lyle ruffled once. That was the time his sister, Clara, put his rifle in her mouth and painted the roughsawn boards in his room with her brains. Generally, he's unflappable: The time his baler caught fire he didn't seem in much of a hurry to put it out.

In this dream he's scared to tears just from being in Denver. He arrives at this house my family lived in for a while. The pickup is loaded down with tape measures of many sizes, all sprung out of their cases. Some are as big as rolls of steel, the way they come from the mill. We start unloading them, but we can't because we are cutting our hands to shreds and we haven't got any gloves. Lyle's eyes are like blue lasers. His tears shine like some light leaking out. Then we are both crying because we can't get the tapes out and Lyle doesn't understand the directions for getting out of the city. I offer to go with him but he refuses, saying things just have too much direction and you can't find your way back to anywhere, and besides, someone has to stay here with the tapes, which have somehow unloaded themselves while we were talking and weeping.

So we shake bloody, shredded hands, both weeping inconsolably because we know that Lyle will never find his way out of the city and back to Sheep Creek, but he is leaving anyway, and I am left standing there with all these tape measures on the lawn of a house where I don't live anymore.

I want to go to Sheep Creek, too, but I can't because of all these tape measures, different sizes, too heavy to lift, too sharp to touch without slicing my fingers into more spaghetti than they already are. I can't even wave good-bye right.

The first owners of the meadow on Sheep Creek (Indians, like I said, never wintered in these mountains) were just hiding out. That's what Lyle says. They weren't really trying to make a go of the place and they didn't. Back then a man could have homesteaded a bigger hay meadow closer to town and down out of the mountains so he wouldn't be buried alive for six months a year. Lyle said, "They were horse thieves or xenophobes or something."

The second name on the deed is App Worster's, a good enough man by plenty to make the place work. He built miles of fences, yards of homemade wooden pipe, a house, barns, sheds, corrals. He put up hay with horses and got down to scythe among the willows where the mower couldn't go. He never quit from last star to first, proving that the price of independence is slavery.

That was before hunting laws and App could harvest what he needed of deer and elk, antelope, grouse, brook trout. Outside the fence around his own meadow there wasn't any fence in those days, so App could turn his cows out in summer and bring them home in winter to feed them the hay he'd made.

What broke App was trying to keep his wives from dying. When one died he married her sister. When the sister died they left four kids and enough doctor bills between them that App had to give up his freedom to stay out of jail.

The third owners weren't even close. They lost the place in the Depression.

White as death and twice as cold, mathematical, it offers itself as a symbol of all stillness, all isolation when it reaches the windowsill and no one is going anywhere for a while, or when, by March, the drifts loom higher than the roofs of houses. The snow is deepest up on Deadman, where all our streams begin, where timber combs the snow out of the wind.

Sometimes in summer the air is so dry the rain evaporates before it reaches the ground. When it rains hard the soil can't take it in. It washes out the roads and pours off the surface of the pasture. Here what living things depend on is the snow that melts off mountain faces and high timber, swelling our springs and streams, filling the reservoir, infusing miles of irrigation ditches, making the meadow green.

Lyle is down mowing. From up here by the cattleguard on the hill, the Farmall looks like a river barge, low in the water, pulling upstream as it makes its first swath through the deep timothy that borders the streak of willows along the creek. The tractor moves forward but Lyle is looking back as he goes, watching the scissoring blades of the sickle bar take down the tall grass. Going forward looking back, spiraling toward the middle of the field.

There's a coyote following the tractor, just about ten feet behind it. Every so often he pops into the air like he's been stung and pounces. He's catching field mice the mower turns up. Lyle isn't paying any attention to him.

A lot of people would shoot a coyote if they got that close to it, which is why a lot of people never get that close. This one isn't Lyle's pet; coyotes can't be tamed, even if you start with a pup. It's as close to a pet as Lyle has, though. He won't have a dog or cat for fear of becoming too attached.

Lyle admires coyotes for more or less the same reasons others hate them. To begin with, the average coyote is smarter than the average human. That is why it's so difficult to trap them, and why they haven't gone the way of wolves. Then there's their toughness and uncompromising independence: if by some lapse in attention one is caught in a trap, off comes the offending limb and he's on his way.

As the price of defiance they have to work harder than most animals just to stay alive. They live mostly on mice and insects. When they are lucky or clever enough to come up with something bigger they are overcome with joy and love for one another. They rhapsodize. They harmonize their loneliness and sorrow and they don't care who likes it.

Lyle says for coyotes, "They sure never pity themselves."

When he gets done mowing he will climb down, choke the tractor, and walk around where that coyote is sitting down just looking at him. He'll chuck a stone or a block of wood at the critter and say, "Don't you know better than to come that close to people?" The coyote, trotting casually away, watching Lyle over his shoulder as he goes, of course, does know better. He knows the difference between this man who lives in the meadow alone, summer and winter, and the ones who set the traps and poisons and poke the muzzles of .30-.30s out the windows of their pickups. This human has somehow raised his consciousness almost up to coyote level.

The coyotes trust Raymond, too, but they must think him sentimental: he puts out Alpo for them. Ray and Lyle can argue all night about the desirability of moose or wolves or grizzlies, but they are in accord on coyotes. Ray says, "You can admire a coyote—he's an outlaw, but it's damned hard to admire a sheep."

Each year when Ray drains the reservoir, trout get stranded in pools below the dam. One August a mother coyote showed up with her two pups to teach them a thing or two about angling, coyote-style. It was before sunrise, but she didn't realize a drunk can be awake anytime, and that morning he surprised them. She somehow let those pups know to run for cover while she held Raymond in her gaze. He tried talking to her, and after awhile, she decided he was harmless if not quite admirable.

The next morning she showed up by the weir in full view of the house. There was the open can of Alpo. Ray was watching, drinking instant coffee, from the kitchen window. After that the three coyotes came in broad daylight. Ray and Margie Worster watched from the house as they splashed and romped in the shallow water, swallowed whole about a bushel of trout apiece, and, bellies swaying, moved off to find some shade in which to spend the rest of the day, and maybe sing a little toward dusk.

The last time Lyle cut hay, before his health gave out, he mowed with the '23 Farmall he bought in 1946, the one he'd used every year for forty years. He gave up haying with horses because horses that are only used one month of the year get too jittery and dangerous. The first field you cut you just have to let them mow where they want to—the swath like a child's scribble in the field. He'd have bought a tractor sooner, but you couldn't during the war.

The Farmall has iron wheels and you have to hand start it choked and with the gas shut off, and then, when it catches, you run like hell back to turn on the gas before it dies. Whenever it broke Lyle fixed it—even if he had to forge a part himself, up in the shop, right in the middle of haying. After a certain point you couldn't buy anything for it anyway. Lyle kept it greased and drove it easy and fixed it when it broke. After about 1960 nothing ever went wrong with it.

In the early years Lyle fixed up a sweep on the front of a truck and ran the hay up with a stacker he made of lodgepole cut nearby. Then the whole family and sometimes neighbors would pitch in. Using a stationary baler, they tied the bales by hand and hauled them to the barn on the 1930 REO, which they also used to haul lumber and sand. That truck is still in the barn in perfect working order, except that you have to drive it down to the creek each day and fill the radiator with the coffee can Lyle keeps under the seat. It leaks exactly one coffee can of water a day whether you drive it or not.

Lyle didn't own any farm equipment newer than 1948. Along with his pickup and car it all belonged in a museum, except that Lyle was too busy using it. That old equipment stopped traffic on the county road at haying time.

Each year for forty years Lyle got the hay into the barn before it started snowing hard, starting in the stubble of the meadow, which disappeared willingly under the first layers of crystals that fell, as if they didn't mean anything by it.

Oscar Marsh, on the other hand, is more of a classic kind of Wyoming rancher. Besides everything else that means, it means if it moves he shoots it. It's like being a ten-year-old with a .22 for your whole life. Nothing changes but the bore. Oscar has a hunting-lodge-style living room with a big stone fireplace in his log house. Some of the most beautiful creatures ever to contain motion are nailed to the wall. It's a kind of innocence, and I don't blame Oscar because he is ninety and pretty leathery himself from all those years in the unrestrained wind.

Once, out riding, Oscar drew a bead on an old coyote at about two hundred yards. As usual he didn't miss. When he rode up to collect the pelt he found that the coyote only had two legs. The other two had been caught in traps at different times in a long and bitter coyote life, and the old bastard had chewed them off, one front foot above the ankle that he could still stump around on, and one hind leg chewed off (or maybe, as Oscar said, shot off) at the knee. Somehow that coyote had figured out how to make a living in his diminished condition. Both wounds were old. His coat was healthy, not starved-looking or mangy. Apparently he was perfectly happy to go on suffering if that's what life was for, though he probably didn't mind being shot by Oscar that much either. Oscar said if he'd known that old boy was missing two legs and still getting along, he didn't know whether he would have shot him or not.

Lyle was born in a house made of dirt. Kind of like a grave with a roof on it. It was dug back into a low hill with slabs of the prairie grass it was lost in piled up high enough in front to support a roof and make a couple of windows so you could look out every once in a while just to make sure there was still absolutely nothing in sight and a door you had to duck under.

Lyle quit school after the eighth grade because his old man ran off and forgot about his three kids and their mother and the sod cabin I'm trying to remember from a photograph I once saw of it. By age fourteen Lyle was able to do a man's work for half a man's wages in the fields, old enough to start killing himself with cigarettes and chew and help his family keep living in the grave they called home.

In Flagler, Colorado, you are too far east to see the mountains, and there are no trees because there is no water. In 1934 it was all dryland farming in what the first Europeans who saw it called a desert. It was the kind of place where you'd think only the poorest most desperate sonofabitch with an overactive imagination and a zealous trust in benevolent powers of a higher nature would even sit down to rest, let alone live, back then, before irrigation turned it green. You'd have to be adaptable as an Eskimo or dumb as a snake to want to call it home.

Sod houses, like jungle huts and igloos, are made from the very stuff the inhabitants seek protection from. It's like fighting fire with fire, only in this case it's fighting grass with grass.

So you start by digging a hole, like a gopher or a prairie dog, then you cut up some of the sod you've disappeared into and sandbag it all around yourself as if there was a nearby river you were expecting to rise, or as if you were making a gun emplacement. You leave a couple of holes for windows and a gap for the door that will be low enough to keep you humble for the rest of your life, even if you move away.

Sod was layered over poles for a roof. The grass on the roof had to be alive to keep the roof from leaking and falling in.

Those burrows were warm and dark in winter, at least a refuge from the raging whiteness that was everything outside. They were like submarines till spring. In summer they were cool, black when you first came in from the bright sunshine. The only real drawbacks were roof leaks and bug-infested walls. The walls could be covered with burlap and whitewashed or plastered white, which stopped the bugs but brought the winter glare inside, a major cause of madness in pioneer women. Lyle's mother never whitewashed their walls and left the burlap dry.

She had three children with her in the grave her husband made for them before he left. Imagine a winter glare. The windows are blank. The house is in a white suspension.

Hear the wind blow.

The doors of sod houses open inward; otherwise, the inhabitants could be trapped by heavy snowfall. After a blizzard the sky is a purple bowl the sun, like an egg, rolls around in. The earth is as blind as a hard cloud. The house is just a slight swell in the snow until someone opens the door inward, and like a drunk who's been leaning there all night, a small avalanche tumbles inside.

From the outside the first thing you see is a broom stuck up out of the snow like a sudden flower. It pokes around, making a hole. Then shovelfuls of snow sail into the air in steady puffs.

One floppy-hatted head pops out from the burrow and, gopherlike, looks all around. Then the whole man climbs out and begins to excavate a passage to the door. Two boys emerge, followed by a smaller boy. They wade out through deep but dry new snow, across the yard to a shedlike affair that is less buried because of the body heat and stamping about of animals.

One boy rolls a bale of hay off the stack to knock the spindrift off it. The other places an icy bucket under the cow and begins to milk with red, swollen hands. The streams of warm milk against the pail sound like fabric ripping. The man unhooks a bridle from a nail and places the bit under his armpit to warm it. The small boy just stands there with his hands at his sides.

When the horse is bridled the man calls to the house the name of a girl or woman, and she emerges from the snow-burrow bundled so tight she can't bend her arms easily. She wears a big, moth-eaten sweater over her coat. She is carrying a ratty green blanket and a lunchbox.

The little boy, who is Lyle, is hoisted onto the horse by

his father and packaged in the blanket. His sister, Clara, hands him the reins and the lunchbox. Lyle begins to flail his heels against the enormous horse's sides without result. This is a horse that wouldn't break into a trot if you dipped his tail in coal oil and lit it. The father says, "Giddyup, Bill," and slaps the horse's flank hard enough to hurt his freezing hand. The horse begins to plod through the smooth, undrifted snow up an almost imperceptible rise toward the deep sky where Lyle disappears on his way to school.

The others, two of whom are not that long out of school themselves, turn back to the snow-mound and disappear inside. The sound the door makes as it shuts is like that of a heavy stone someone dropped to the ground after carrying it a long way. By now a thread of smoke rises straight as steel pipe from the dwelling into the still sky.

There are six children in the one-room school. The floor is dirt and the air smells of coal smoke. The walls are not sod like all the children's houses but made from logs hauled all the way from the foothills of the Rockies. The school perches fully above the ground. It reminds Lyle of a birdhouse. The children are obedient. The schoolmarm is kindly and crazy as the wind. The children study hard because they know it's their last chance to learn something before they become useful as labor to their families.

Lyle, though he doesn't know it yet, will be working in the fields with his brothers this summer, trying to do a man's share, because his father has already decided to leave for good as soon as the first flowers spatter the pasture.

Lyle sits alone during lunch because he is embarrassed by his sandwiches, which are made from homemade bread, the badge of poverty. The other kids have Sunbeam. School ends early on winter days so the children have time to walk or ride home before dark.

When Lyle reaches home he gives the horse some hay and grain. He rubs the horse down with straw, not because it is in a sweat (it isn't), but because he thinks the horse likes it and it's something to do instead of going inside. From the house he can hear his father screaming at his mother with the kind of lunacy that infects prairie dwellers in winter. Lyle thinks the really smart creatures know enough to sleep till spring.

So he stays out in the shed with the animals, trying to keep warm between the horse and the cow. He is not waiting to be called for supper; they won't call him. He is waiting for his teeth to chatter so hard he's afraid they'll break.

When we think of our lives as what we have done, memory becomes a museum with one long shelf on which we arrange a bric-a-brac of deeds, each to his own liking. Lyle doesn't think of his life as what he has done, or what was done to him. He has no use for blame. The day his father left for good never came to an end. His mother tried to hide her relief, which was a joy that came over her like tough spring flowers in fearless colors flushing the high plains that winter leaves so female for a while.

Between the floating blankness of winter and the monotonous, burnt-out summer tones, the quick thrill of color over the dusty flats was just how she felt that spring. And that's how fast it was gone—faster. Her husband's labor had made more difference than she ever would have admitted to him. Now they couldn't afford to stay where they were and they couldn't afford to leave. So they left. I think the reason Hazel decided to go was because she knew her two oldest sons would leave home if she didn't take them away herself. It was her attempt to keep them with her.

They moved to Boulder a hundred miles west, which was, at the time, a humble farming town slumped in a foothill valley so close to the mountains you couldn't see them from town: the first little ridge to the west blocks out the higher peaks, making proximity to the high country oddly plain and comforting.

They rented a tiny bungalow on the outskirts of town. They kept chickens, pigs, and milk cows. The two older boys hired on to road crews, did welding and auto repair in the winter, got farm work in July. They blistered their ears and noses and dizzied their brains under felt hats driving tractors or teams pulling combines and headers in circles.

They spent no money except for food and cigarette makings, the occasional new hat or pair of overalls ("overhauls," Lyle called them). Hazel wanted to send Lyle back to school in the fall. She wanted him to learn a trade, make a steady wage, which sounded good to Lyle, but it never came about.

Clara made a little money painting landscapes from photographs—people's houses or favorite mountain views—a talent she had discovered early in the grueling bleakness of prairie winters. Hazel did the housework and cooking, some tailoring and mending for families in town, and stayed up many nights ripping the seams out of her sons' bluejeans and sewing the un-worn-out backs of pants over the fronts of other pairs worn out at the knees, restitching the seams on her treadle Singer. Each pair of jeans lasted half again as long that way. Hazel also mended their torn shirts and worn-out shoes, darned socks, and pieced quilts from scraps of clothing too far gone to mend. She wasted nothing, or to be more precise, she wasted no things.

The whole family worked with a ferocity and inventiveness that could only have been provided by an intelligent woman who had spent her life till now stranded halfway, who'd had enough of living in a house made of dirt, surrounded by measureless prairies of dirt, pulling food from the dirt to feed to her sons who were covered with the same dirt they all worked, ate, and slept in. She started hoarding a portion of the money they got, saving fiercely, wasting nothing, buying nothing new and nothing at all they could make themselves or do without, pretending to nothing.

Her children got nothing for themselves, any more than she did. They lived for a better future she would reveal to them. They were humble and hardworking as the earth itself, the dry earth of the prairie.

During the Depression most families were slipping, losing land and possessions. Hazel was holding ground, even gaining a little. She was already an expert at the kind of poverty the rest of the country was just beginning to learn and would never master.

Lyle was fourteen and old enough to think that a man had a right to one thing, at least, in life, one simple pleasure, which was to stop killing himself every so often for long enough to sprinkle a few golden flakes of crimp-cut tobacco into a delicate boat of paper, held just so between thumb, index, and middle finger, to roll it and lick it and strike a wooden kitchen match to light it and go back to work with the cigarette stuck to his lower lip.

And sometimes, at noon or sundown, the ritual included the possibility of sitting down long enough to smoke it, too. Life had three parts: working from first light to last, sleeping too tired to dream, so deep he was pretty sure he knew what death was like, and smoking cigarettes.

Eating didn't count because the food was so plain it was part of work, like pouring gasoline in a tractor. Lyle never took pleasure in eating, any more than a coyote would.

In the Depression a lot of people lost their lives, if your life is what you do. People who had never missed a mortgage payment, had worked hard, not for money but for a way of life, lost their land when its value dropped below the amount they owed. Old story.

The illusion of land ownership creates a cheap workforce in the fields: people who often pay more than they are paid to work, as we say, like slaves. But, oh, they are rich in illusions of independence, and they are also very proud, which is not an illusion.

In 1938 Hazel Van Waning was not in a position to feel sorry for anyone. She assumed the loan, $2,000 remaining—a song, Lyle called it—on a small mountain farm: 320 acres of hay meadow in a valley surrounded by so much green it was hard to imagine winter ever being there, though it was precisely winter at that elevation (8,500 ft.) and that far from town that made it so no one in his right mind would actually try to *live* there. A few families who were not in their right minds had tried and failed to keep a grip on it, one of them App Worster's.

Hazel didn't feel sorry for him, either. In fact, feeling sorry, that questionable human capacity, for herself or anyone else, was something she would never regain, not even in relative comfort, not in this life.

She didn't believe in borrowing so she bought the deed outright, in cash, from a banker who was amazed to have unloaded a backwoods property he thought he was stuck with. The bank clerks made jokes about the woman who had given all her savings to acquire a piece of land not only unprofitable but untenable, and her without a husband to work the land for her. They were laughing about it when

27

word came down that the bank was folding and all the laughing employees were no longer employed.

Hazel signed the deed in '38, but she kept her family in Boulder, all of them working at something. They were poorer that year than they ever had been. Lyle hired on to the road crew where his brother, Bob, was already working. They were mostly over near South Park, building fence along the new highway. They were supposed to drive steel posts a uniform depth along the new road so that the white painted tops came out looking even. Some of the posts wouldn't go that deep into the rocky ground, so it fell to Lyle, the newest and youngest member of the crew, to cut off the tops of the high posts with a hacksaw and repaint them when the foreman wasn't looking.

All the wages the boys brought in went to fixing up the dilapidated log cabin and caved-in sheds that were evidence of grim failures on the farm they'd bought. Slowly the place became livable. They soon bought a team to hay the meadow and fixed the barbed wire fence around its perimeter, cutting their own posts and piecing together short lengths of wire they scavenged where snowdrifts and elk snapped the fence each winter.

The house itself was well made, if neglected. A log house lasts forever in this climate as long as it has a good roof over it and a foundation under it. In 1940, Hazel moved her family up to Sheep Creek for good. The cabin had three rooms: two bedrooms and an everything-else room with a wood cookstove and a wood heater.

Henry joined the Army that year and learned to fly: Hazel's nightmare. He figured she had Lyle and Bob to work for her and Clara to chew on all day, and it seemed like now or never, so off he went in his green uniform, and none of them ever saw him again.

In February of 1941 the snow rose past the windowsills. The family tried to make the best of what looked like the cold tunnel of the rest of their lives. Bob promised to build snowfences the next summer so they wouldn't be buried alive like that again. He and Lyle spent the winter nights shivering in the unheated lean-to they'd built on the back of the house. Clara took a snapshot with the family's Brownie of the snowdrift in front of the house. She perched her own wool hat on top of it and placed sticks with her mittens on them so it looked like someone buried in the snow and reaching for air. With a pen she drew an arrow on the print pointing to the hat and wrote, *ME*, and sent it to a friend in Boulder. Hazel showed them how, as a girl in Iowa, when hoarfrost grew thick as ferns on the windows, she'd heat a thimble on the stove and use it to melt a peephole in the frost, to spy on the still, white world outside.

The problem is there is no one to blame for this. It's just so much snow you can't see. It's just a blizzard like white ants moving in mild waves and stopping, covering, moving on, covering everything, moving on, uncovering and covering everything again, getting deeper, the wind ordering and disordering and ordering them to advance, stop, advance, wait; or like an invasion of angels. Advance, stop, advance, wait, so that they all move forward like a wave, but they are never all moving together like a wave, claiming, reaching, deepening, and you can't see. If you could rise above and look down on this blindness you might see that the whole storm is a kind of silence.

From up there you could see a Model-A car that has lost its top, as if it were decked out for a sunny Sunday drive, and the leather seats look as if they are covered with white mold, and then they fill, and there is a delicate mantle of snow, like an eyebrow, on top of the steering wheel, in the lee of the windshield, and at first you can see the last of the deep ruts the narrow tires cut in the snow before the snow got higher than the axles and the wheels just spun in place. The ruts are filling fast. They resemble unsure lines drawn by a hand that lifted off the page while drawing, gesturing disappearance, and in the time it took to say that they have disappeared.

The point of view can't rise high enough to find the edge of the storm. The car fills and is lost to the principle of whiteness, blankness, stupidity and, without the car, the point of view is also lost, without external reference or direction. It could be spinning. You wouldn't know.

It's only logical to think there must be people somewhere near, a way to explain, someone to blame for the abandonment of the car. There must always be an explanation for abandonment, a destination maybe. The point of view wants someone to blame for this, somewhere to pin the cause and effect. It needs reasons. It wants to give these people, whose car has foundered, a home to try to get to, even in this storm. Because you have to make assumptions. Because you have to assume they do not want to die, or they do not want to want to, or some of them are helping others in not wanting.

Down there: a footprint like a posthole in the snow. The footprint is filling up, full, gone, but there is another one not yet quite full, which provides a sense of direction. Back off. A bit left. There they are.

There are four people. One slogs ahead through knee-deep drifts, leaning into them like a horse leaning into the harness. The others follow carefully, saving their strength by placing their feet in the foot holes of the first. They look like majorettes in slow motion, prancing, but not a joyful kind of prancing and not a proud kind. No one is having fun. A little closer.

The old man whose full white beard is filled with spindrift breaks trail. The three that follow are his sons. He blames himself for everything, even though it is just October. He has icicles of tobacco juice dangling like a nasty chandelier from the whiskers under his lower lip. With every steam engine puff of breath he breathes a curse against himself in rhythm with each slogging step.

He does not curse the freak fall storm any more than he would curse an invasion of angels. In counterpoint to his own poisonous huffing, he hears the breathing of his eldest son, then the lighter breaths of Ray, the middle one, and a little farther behind again, the toneless grace notes of the youngest, who stumbles often and they have to stop and wait for him. It's taking longer for him to get up each time. How the old man hears these small sounds above or below the screech of wind cannot be explained. He just hears them, and his hearing ties them together in the whiteout like a thick rope between prisoners of war or kindergarten children on a busy street.

When Jack, the smallest, falls and can't get up again, the old man, App, stops making posthole tracks. Pete, the oldest, bumps blindly into his father's back, and then he, too, sits down in the snow. Ray shouts, "Jack won't get up, Dad. He says he wants to take a nap."

The wind cheers louder.

Appleton Worster, twice a widower, stops mid-furrow in the snow. He tilts back his head as if to laugh, but he isn't laughing. His sky-blue eyes veer wildly upward in doubtful surprise and it's more of a grimace, like apostles wear in paintings of the Crucifixion.

"Dad," Ray says, and then louder, as if App were the one threatening to fall asleep, "Dad! Come help wake up Jack. He'll get cold if he don't wake up now. He's got snow all over him and he's starting to take a nap."

App lowers his eyes, breathes in, and spits out a stream of tobacco juice that blows back into his beard like a flyline cast into the wind. Then he circles back to where his youngest son is splayed out on his back and says, "Get up, you little harelip runt," and lifts him up by the collar of the oversized brown wool coat that both of his brothers have worn and outgrown, lifts him up like a pup that has made a deliberate mess and is about to be heaved out the door by the scruff of his neck. App turns him around and delivers a serious kick to Jack's skinny ass and says, "Get along, dammit, or we'll none of us get home." And he does.

Imagine again the aerial view, the four figures pulling single file through the dry, feathery, now thigh-deep snow. It has snowed three feet in sixteen hours. Now Pete goes first, making more of a slow motion wake than tracks. Ray goes second, towing his little brother by one coat sleeve, which has by now pulled down from his thin arm like the empty sleeve of an amputee and has twisted the coat around and halfway off. App brings up the rear in two senses, heaving back and giving Jack a good kick about every twenty steps or if the youngster stops and says he's sleepy, whichever comes first.

33

"I'm sleepy, Dad," and he jolts forward two or three trip-steps and starts slogging again. They look like figures in a cartoon: each of the old man's kicks juices them forward a few paces and they stop again, bumping into each other, and then another kick. But it isn't a cartoon. It's real, it's true. Though it might have irony, the truth is never funny.

After another hour of crippling along just so, the blizzard's white is traded for equal depth of blackness. Night without the sky. App is no longer sure where they are, but figures they have to keep going. At a certain point you keep going to see what happens next.

Maybe, eventually, they will strike some feature of the landscape App recognizes: a rock outcrop or fenceline. But how to tell one fence from another in this night and weather? He wants to pick up the little boy in his arms, but he knows if Jack stops moving he will freeze. His mind wanders, more aimless, but not as lost as he has gotten himself and his boys.

He thinks of his own father, whom everyone, including App, agreed was a mean, useless old shit. He'd been a sea captain out of Maine and had crossed the prairie west in the early years, never again to smell salt air. He never quit talking about how hard it was to navigate that vast, featureless landscape awash in grass. He had sold his mariner's instruments never thinking how badly he would want them back in South Dakota.

They had to travel during the day to keep from wrecking wagon wheels, hitting stones and falling into washes. At night he reckoned as best he could from the wheeling stars. During the day they trailed a length of rope and watched it to keep themselves heading straight. Going forward looking back. If the rope started to snake, they'd heave to and snake it back, as if they were trying to get away from it though it was fastened to them, and they needed that rope, not tying them to anything, to find their way.

App remembers how his father always spoke of how they

"landed" at Diamond Peak on the Colorado-Wyoming border, which always seemed funny to App since there'd been nothing but land for months. Hell, they'd been *at land* the way sailors are *at sea*, adrift in grass as he and his sons were adrift in a sea of black snow, only he didn't remember any of it since he'd made the crossing in his mother's arms.

"Hey," Pete shouts from the darkness ahead, "there's a cliff up here."

"Does it rise or fall?" App yells back.

"It goes up."

App spits, relieved they aren't rimrocked. Better not to be on something you could fall off. He leaves Ray holding Jack by the sleeve and wades up to where Pete waits. App stops and sniffs like a grizzly bear, and a smell he hates gives him the first good feeling he's had all day. Even in this cold and wind he can smell it: the pungent, resinous, musty stink of a packrat's nest.

"Now we'll be fine, boys."

Ray puts in hopefully, "Now do you know where we are?"

"Yep. Right here."

App scrambles up onto a snow-covered ledge and pulls the boys up after him, one by one by their collars, now like a mother lynx moving her kits. Here at least they are out of the wind. App crawls back along the ledge, following the smell that would have tightened his throat if it weren't so cold, back into a crevice where the packrats have built and abandoned a nest of finger-width sticks covered with their own varnishlike piss.

"Nobody home. Get that cracker-assed kid up here," App says, fishing a match from his coat pocket and lighting it with the thumbnail of the same hand that holds the match—the same one-handed flourish he uses to light the kerosene lamps at home. The boys watch as fire springs from their father's hand. As the sticks catch they begin to feel the heat on their windburned faces.

"Did I ever tell you the story . . ." App begins, and as he does his mind feels to him like a packrat balanced on a stringer in the barn, sluggishly feinting back and forth, firmly in the sights of some ranch kid's .22. Two bad choices: stay huddled here in the rocks and rest—he knows how long that nest will burn, not very; or strike out again when the fire wanes, into the storm that seems bound to lose them. He thinks the boys will be more frightened if they stay.

The idea of their being scared, of their knowing how bad things really are, depresses the old man and shames him. His depression and shame scare the hell out of him. He knows that under circumstances in which well-being is not a possibility, the illusion of well-being is a matter of life and death. And what if he gets them all confounded, leads them away from the safety of home? When he thinks of the cabin, probably colder inside than out by now, with its stove stone-cold, dirt floor, and no mother to hustle them in and warm them with soup and coffee, he thinks, why fight it. Then he kicks himself mentally the way he's been kicking Jack all afternoon to keep him from freezing . . . no, to keep him alive even though he was freezing. He sees Ray's eyes drooping.

". . . of the time your old granddad and me was up on Deadman Mountain hunting deer and elk meat for the town of Laramie?" He knows they've heard it to death so he doesn't wait for an answer. Just as well kill them with boredom as let them freeze, he thinks, but they wouldn't answer anyway because it was their favorite story and they didn't want to lie.

"I'd loaned my rifle, the old .44-.40 to a sheepherder who'd had coyote trouble, but now I'd got it back, so that when I woke up that morning and looked across the clearing where we'd camped and saw that curious old grizzly sniffing us out, standing up on his hind legs with his nose up in the air and his front paws hanging limp so that he looked just like a overgrowed gopher, I thought I'd just as well shoot him since he'd volunteered. I mean he was just about *begging* me to shoot him, standing up like that with those little gopher paws.

"So I reached back and grabbed my rifle and said, 'Wake up, Dad,' just before I squeezed the shot off so's I wouldn't scare the old sonofabitch to death without waking him up first.

"The first shot wasn't bad, but it was a lung shot and that bear changed from a giant gopher into a full-fledged, madder-than-hell grizzly and came after me across that clearing with blood more or less pouring out of his mouth.

"But I wasn't worried, boys, hell no. I figured I was the one with the rifle. I took careful aim for a head shot and just as he jumped on me I fired. Only I didn't fire. I just kind of clicked. The rifle had jammed on me. That bear had just enough strength left to clamp on to my thigh and hang on to see which one of us died first and which one second. By now I was starting to worry. I couldn't move. I had this not-completely-dead grizzly bear hanging off my leg. I thought I was pretty young and tough, like you boys are, but I was afraid that bear would find the strength to finish biting off my leg before he died.

"Well, by then my old man was getting pretty well waked up and was coming around the tent with the double-bitted axe in his hands. 'Roll over, App, so's I can get him a decent lick,' he said about as calm as high noon in July.

"Well, boys, have you ever tried to roll over with a grizzly bear clamped to your leg? Steel jaws anchored to about eight hundred pounds of meat—now that's what I call a bear trap. Well, I tried it and I can tell you it hurt some, but I rolled over just enough and Dad raised that axe over his head and split that bear skull off my thigh just like he was splitting wood for the kitchen stove."

As App spins out the familiar tale, his mind still clambers back and forth over what is best to do. He watches his sons' faces, red and chapped from windburn and riveted in the fireglow as if they were sitting around a campfire on a summer fishing trip. At least he'd get their minds off where they are, which is mostly what stories are good for anyway.

"I still carry the scars to this day," he says, and they know it's true, since they've seen those scars, like raindrops in dust, a thousand times, more times than they've heard the story.

"From that day I resolved never to loan a firearm to anyone, lessen it was a matter of life and death, number one, and number two, to learn to handle the double-bitted axe as good as my sourpussed old man, which I done."

When the story ends they all hear the wind again. Their grim present starts pushing back in, taking back what's left of the fire, and the little space the story made. Fear invades the children's faces like cloud shadows rising on the side of a cliff. Then Ray says, "Do you know where we are?" and App's mind begins again that rodentlike back and forth between the truth his sons expect of him, and the lie that might give them enough hope to save them. The packrat nest is down to coals and ash. It is getting time to decide a few things.

"I guess this is no place for kids," App says, and then he thinks no place ever is. "Come on, we're almost home," he says, and then he thinks, *either way*. He says, "We don't want to be late."

Ray listened to the story of his father and his father's father and the bear. He heard it as if it were traveling a long distance to reach him, from beyond his father's voice, as if the story had existed before his father and his father's father had been born. It was like a Bible story he'd heard from Miss Gunnerson at school, one of those where fathers and sons somehow love each other through veils of rage and God's mean tricks. That could never happen to Ray. God seemed to more or less leave them alone, compared to doings in the Bible, and Ray loved his father with a distillate of admiration and trust so pure it would shrivel the Devil if you sprinkled it on him. The awful-smelling twigs of the burning nest flamed down, glowed, and changed to ash that briefly held the selfsame form before snowing down in a heap.

He studied the faces of his brothers and father that were like the faces of a tiny, motherless tribe of terrified savages. All their wet wool clothes were steaming as if their souls were already rising, before they even died. The heat felt good, but it was fast going. Ray looked down at his own felt-lined denim coat that was sending up a junglelike mist wreathing about his head. His wool cap was also steaming; the cuffs of his trousers were frozen solid as sections of stovepipe. He looked up and saw his father's face, framed by the flowing beard, white, but tobacco-stained so that it was like granite streaked with lichen.

App, in fact, had so much beard that mostly what one noticed was the blueness of his eyes, which Ray had been told more than once were exactly like his own, though he had only seen himself in a mirror maybe a dozen times in his life. Right now he couldn't remember what he looked like. He tried, but he couldn't picture himself. He just hoped he still had his father's eyes, that distant color, like a mountain so far off at first you think it's just sky.

Pete had his mother's eyes, but Ray knew that only from what his father said. Ray never knew Pete's mother, and the few photographs they had of her showed her far away, for instance in the doorway of the cabin App built that burned down, on the ranch he used to have that was a green meadow surrounded by timbered hills. App lost the ranch when she was sick for so long and needed so many doctors and she died anyway.

She was standing in that doorway holding Pete's older sister, who also died. When he looked into Pete's eyes he thought there was something dead about them, too, because they were his mother's, and they were a vegetal green, almost brown. Other than that Ray thought Pete looked aristocratic, like a president or something, with a strong chin and straight nose, a face you'd see on money or stamps, a Roman emperor or somebody rich.

Ray looked at Jack, who was shivering quietly. Jack had been born with a cleft palate and harelip, which his long pointy nose drooped over. No one but Ray could understand him when he spoke, and there was no doubt about it, he looked like hell. Ray got into fistfights almost daily at school, when they got to school, because other boys made fun of Jack, who was too puny to defend himself and cried easily.

A shiver went through Ray when App said it was time to move again, and he was afraid for his little brother. Ray often felt that he loved Jack more for his weakness and terrible looks than he might have otherwise, but he couldn't figure why that should be. App said he was soft-hearted and Ray could never tell if that was good or bad. He thought it was probably bad. Well, if App said they'd get home there was nothing to worry about, because App knew everything, though it might be hard and take a long time.

One by one App lifted them down and said, "Come on, boys. We've got a piece to go, and I want to get to bed tonight. Ray, grab hold of Jack again, and Pete, you shove him from behind when he needs it." Then he turned and plowed into the snow again like a tugboat leaving the harbor.

As it turned out they were indeed not far from home. The snow stopped with eerie suddenness. The wind quit working on them. Suddenly the whole thing seemed like the jokes kids played on Jack at school, the kind that make you mad. The stars showed like holes drilled in a tin roof beyond which it was always day. The outline of Boulder Ridge proclaimed itself. It looked too big ever to lose.

When they reached the cabin App lit the heater and a piece of the matchhead stuck under his thumbnail and flared there, but he didn't mention it. He tossed on a piece of split pitch pine, and they stood around the ticking metal box waiting for the steam to start rising off them again.

App took Jack in his arms and wrapped him under his own coat, waiting. Pete lit the lamp. The glass chimney was streaked with smoke, but in its light Ray could see the tears begin to stream down his father's face. Tears dripped from the ends of his moustache like water off the eaves after the rain stops falling and fell into his son's hair that was the color of late summer grass.

Ray hardly took notice of this, since he had seen his father cry often before at inexplicable times and he was used to not knowing why.

According to scientists who study avalanches for a living, snow has the widest range of physical properties of any known substance. What's amazing is that the Eskimo language doesn't have *more* words for it. Powder snow, corn snow, sugar snow, windpack. Neve, slab, spring powder, spit, and fluff. Thawing and freezing it changes with every degree of temperature, every passing second. Goose down, ball bearings, broken styrofoam.

Then there are the properties of snow that are not physical, or not exactly physical: its lethal whims, its harmlessness, its delicacy, its power, its relentlessness, its flirtatious disregard, its sublime beauty.

Harmless enough, the season's first flakes arrive in the stubble of the mown field, in the spiked branches of pines. They vanish in the morning sun as though they never meant anything by it. And what do they mean in midwinter when the hard-packed drifts settle in, oppressing the foreseeable future? A little wind and spindrift makes them smolder.

All winter the drifts come and go. They have a sense of direction, but they aren't going anywhere. The flakes come straight down or sideways, fast or slow; sometimes they don't fall but swirl and hover and take off like swallows. The meadow fills, and drifts make bridges over the fences. Everybody waits.

The fences break under the weight of so much beauty. Who does the meadow belong to now? For half the year it belongs to the snow, not a thing you can do with it, and by April no one thinks it's pretty anymore, though it is.

Lyle said, "If you want to know who really owns your

land, don't pay the taxes for a while. Then if you want to know who owns it even more, just look out the window in a blizzard. That's the landlord's face looking in, snooping."

Ray, who didn't own any land and never had, outside the lot his doublewide was on in Laramie, thought of snow as a beautiful way to die.

CLARA, 1949

1/1 I started two new pictures. Lyle put up his stove in the cabin.

1/2 I cleaned up around the house. Tried to fix hole where packrat got in. Lyle went to ditch camp AM, worked in shop PM. It's cold and snowing all day.

1/3 Woke up this AM still blizzarding. 10 below. Willis won't get home today.

1/4 Still a blizzard all day. Lyle braved it up to the ditch camp. Two above zero. Shows signs of letting up tonight.

1/5 At last it cleared up and the sun shown most of the day. Lyle worked in the shop. I painted. Mom read.

1/6 Another beautiful day. Mom and I cleaned chicken house. Spent all morning outdoors.

1/7 Cold again today. Wind came up from the east. Lyle visited Pat in PM. They looked with Pat's spyglass. No one out to Marsh's yet. Plains sure white.

1/8 Wind and blizzard from the east again today. Not so bad as before, not so much snow, but plenty cold. I did some painting. Lyle worked in the shop. Two more pictures done.

1/9 Mom did some sewing today. I painted.

1/10 I washed. Pat was over to dinner. Beautiful day. We had target practice with Pat's pistol. I shot my clothesline in two—clothes all down in the snow.

1/11 Another beautiful day. We all went over to Pat's for dinner. Took camera along, got some pictures. Found out Bill and Elbertine got back just yesterday, horseback.

1/12   Bill and Elbertine came down about 10:30 AM. Bill and Lyle butchered. Had a nice visit with them. Pretty fair day. Wind in east but warm.

1/13   Lyle, Pat, and Bill opened road to mailbox. Mom and I cut willows and smoked meat and I ironed.

1/14   Lyle, Pat, and Bill went to town. I painted. Turned cold and stormy.

1/15   I did some more painting. Lyle worked in the shop. Stayed cold all day. Down to eighteen below tonight.

1/16   It's clear AM. West wind and 2 above.

1/17   Lyle went over to Pat's to see about going to mailbox. Wind blew snow too bad. They didn't go. I painted.

1/18   Mom sewing a shirt. Lyle working in shop making a beautiful stationery chest. I sewed most all day. Made a new dress.

1/19   It's cold and snowing again today.

1/20   Snowy, cold, east wind.

1/21   I washed today. Lyle busy in the shop on some new project. It snowed an inch or so, sun shone at noon.

1/22   I wrote a letter, did some painting. It snowed some more.

1/23   Still cold, staying by the fire. Painting, reading. Lyle making a metal lathe these days.

1/24   Lyle spent AM digging out. Little warmer. Everyone busy inside. I brought out my watercolors. Made a fairly nice picture. Radio said our mail was at Marsh's.

1/25   Lyle went to Pat's and headed for mailbox. Mom and I cleaned the henhouse, dug out rye stack. Windy and snow blowing, but sun shining.

1/26 Been cold, wind blowing day and night. 4 below this AM, wind still blowing. So much electricity it puts the radio completely out.

1/27 More snow, little warmer. Wind left us a quiet night. I made a note box. Lyle still working on lathe, scooped a "ton" of snow out of the barn.

1/28 Wind!? began again after breakfast. What a day. Mom wrote letters, I sewed an underskirt. Lyle worked on the feeder and a while in the shop.

1/29 Did I say wind?! It was worse today. But it did get a little warmer. I patched overalls, we wrote letters.

1/30 Got up to 36 today but !-#?@ the wind! And what new snowdrifts overnight! Bill and Elbertine spent the day. I scooped out the chickenhouse doors.

1/31 Most awful cold and wind still at it. I put in the day painting. Mom sewed. Lyle and Bill went to town even though it was zero or 10 above all day. They went right over the snowdrifts.

5/16 Beautiful day today. Bob went to College rodeo. Lyle went to town and brought back two little pigs. I make picture frames.

5/17 Lyle repairing branding chute, Bob irrigating. Mom and I finish garden, clean springbox, hang screen door.

5/18 Boys brand, de-horn AM, fix fence PM. I work on Marie's chair, Mom cleans wallpaper.

5/19 I washed and baked cookies. Mom baked bread. Boys took tractor up to sawmill and started skidding logs.

5/20 Boys worked in timber, skidding logs.

5/21   Lyle worked in shop. Bob and Mom went to Marsh's AM. Bob brought back horse to break. I'm ironing.

5/22   Boys irrigating, hauling lumber, getting horses out of Pat's. Williams brought cattle today. Mom and I take Elbertine down on Sand Creek and picked gooseberries.

8/2   Mom and I pick strawberries AM. Went down toward Sand Creek PM picked more ripe gooseberries. Bob still gone. Lyle worked on welder. Mom canned 10 pts. strawberry jam.

8/3   Mom and I canned 8 more qts. of ripe gooseberries, made 4 pts. jelly. Picked more strawberries. Bob mowed hay across creek. Lyle made repairs to tires, etc. Made search for porcupine. Munds came for strawberries.

8/4   Started for town. Found Rhoda and dudes were coming for another pic-nic so came home. Rained so ate indoors. Bob trying to mow hay.

8/5   Went to town. Bob mowing hay, Lyle sharpening sickles.

8/6   I clean house, can strawberries Mom picked. Made 8 pts. Bob mowing hay. Mom gone to cook for Edith's hay crew.

8/7   Mom didn't get home till 4 PM. Boys got ½ day mowing done, rained out. I went to see Elbertine PM. We went with Bill up by Slick Rock. He fished, we looked for moonshine cabin.

10/1   Bob was skidding logs till the horses drug him over one—broke a rib. Lyle spent half day building cattleguard, then took Bob to town.

10/2 Mom and I mix cement, chink scratch shed. Lyle cut wood. Bob went to mailbox.

10/3 Roberts was here at noon. Said they were coming right over to help bale hay. Bob gone back to town for help at the sawmill but no luck. Dick helped Lyle saw.

10/4 No hay balers. Bob and Lyle hauled down load lumber. Axford came, brought 4,180 lbs. barley, got load of lumber. I did some chinking, sewed curtains.

10/5 It cleared this AM. Mom and I went to town. Got to see and hear Thomas Dewey, "the next President of the U.S.". Took McM. their mail.

10/6 Cold rain, snow. I ironed. Lyle and Alferd put up snow fence. Bob finally rented a baler.

10/7 Bob gone for gas, wire, baler. Lyle and Alferd went for Johnson's tractor. Got set to bale.

10/8 Started baling. Got one stack. McMurray's, Bob and I went to dance at Virginia Dale.

10/9 I washed, washed my hair. Boys started to bale. Got two men from Roberts, then baler blew up.

10/10 Bob went to Ft. Collins for new gears. Got head for tractor, sold load of hay. I ironed. Mom dug turnips. Lyle and Alferd hauled a load of lumber, built baler blocks.

10/11 Dick helped bale hay till 3:00, I helped tie. Long, a horse buyer, and Slim Weeks all came at noon, hold up the works. Bob went to town eve. brought out three men.

10/12 Sure get the hay baled today. Cloudy, windy, raining tonight.

10/13 Finished baling hay in the snow.

. . .

11/8   Seven inches of snow. Boys brought saw belts and team home. I spent the day painting. It's cold, it's winter now. . . .

App's leg felt like it was bandaged in barbed wire instead of his own shredded underwear. The wagon was heaped with deer and elk carcasses and hides, salted between the layers, so full that his old man had to walk while App, who couldn't walk much, drove the wagon. Usually it was App who walked, and, despite the circumstance, the old man was getting angrier with every mile. App could hear him back there cursing under his breath and spitting. When the old man let loose with a jet of tobacco it sounded like piss on hot coals.

Coming down from the mountain known as Deadman the trail curved and contoured, maintaining its elevation on the mountainside as it followed the creek that hissed below. Then it threaded through a small stand of timber and began to sidle downhill. A stone under a wagon wheel here could dump the entire load into the frantic creek two hundred feet below.

They rumbled smoothly through the trees, which mapped the horses' backs in sunlight and shade until they emerged onto open talus where the trail steepened and narrowed to negotiate a recent rockslide. Suddenly the horses caught the scent of something they didn't care for—neither man ever saw what it was—and they shied and bolted, the fist-sized stones in the trail sending tooth-shattering shockwaves through the spindly wooden wheels (the springs were loaded down so that the wagon bed rested directly on the axle blocks). App reined in, wishing that his father had gotten oxen or at least mules for this, then the outside rear wheel splintered and the wagonful of once swift and beautiful bodies swung sideways off the trail and the rear end of the wagon swung like a compass needle pointing down at the magnetic tumble of the creek.

App went from reining in as hard as he could to whip-cracking and whooping and urging, trying to use the remaining momentum and the horses' adrenaline to regain the trail, or at least not to loose the entire salt-and-bloody cargo into the creek below, which was all he could hear, or was that just blood rushing through his head?

He managed to keep three wheels on the trail, but the back of the wagon was cattywhampus, and one rear wheel was toothpicks and a hoop.

When the moment ebbed and the horses stilled and the situation bespoke itself in the silence that followed (even the creek's roar was a silence now), the silence issuing from the old man overwhelmed it, and the creek became a noise again, and the roaring in App's ears came out of it, and all the sounds together became the sound of his father's wrath building. App knew what was coming so he just sat there waiting, still as granite, not from fear but from a calm prescience of the inevitable. Without turning he heard the old man's breathing and the crunch of his boots punishing the gravel. He felt the back end of the wagon lift perceptibly, which was not what he was expecting, so he craned around to see the old man squatted down behind the wagon, heaving-to in a carnival-like attempt to lift the impossible back onto the road.

App stared in amazement for a full thirty seconds as his father strained under the load, which indeed he could move, but which no mortal could lift. The cords in his neck went taut, his face reddened, his eyes bulged, sweat sprang from his brow. App wondered if a man could explode himself, split his own skull open like that bear skull split by the axe. He had time to think, "I hope the old shit blows up now because when he finds out he can't lift a ton of literally dead weight, he'll still have strength to kill me with a handy boulder or wheel shard, even though it was me kept the whole works from upsetting and it wasn't me spooked the horses, which should have been oxen that stop stock-still when they spook, and now we'll have to unload the whole mess anyway—*I* will if I ain't dead by then and here he comes."

App felt himself lifted by the shirt and trousers like a marionette, up off the seat, and then he was airborne, sailing down the talus slope toward the creek, and the old man yelling, "Damn you, anyway."

App knew from breaking colts that the best thing to do while flying through the air is to relax, so when he crumpled among the boulders he was no more bruised than he would have been from an ordinary beating at his father's hands, and he thanked the stars for that. The toothmarks in his thigh still hurt more than the cuts and bruises, so he thought about how easy he'd got off as he set to work unloading the wagon, and his father even helped him lift with pry poles to where they could replace the wheel with a drag stick wedged like half a travois into the axle.

By the time they were loaded again it was almost dark and there was no hope of reaching town that night. Driving the horses on those rocky trails in the dark was too risky, and they felt as if they'd had enough catastrophe for one hunting trip. So instead of heading down Sand Creek for Laramie the old man had App steer around the sidehill toward Sheep Creek drainage. He knew of a low spot where they could lay over. The cold air that hung down there nights would keep the meat ten or twenty degrees colder so they might have something besides hides to sell when they finally reached Laramie.

Where they turned the hill was just below where the Wilson Ditch now lifts water out of Sand Creek and carries it around the hill into Sheep Creek and Eaton Reservoir. By the time they descended into the meadow App could feel the cold air already pooling there. He could not see that the meadow was ringed with low timbered ridges. There was no moon and it was full dark when they bottomed out. He smelled willow bushes and mint.

They dropped down into the trapped cold, and App shivered, more than from cold, but he didn't know what. They hobbled the horses near the creek. They wrapped themselves in one blanket and slept under the wagon.

Sometimes the winter sun is so hot coming through the south-facing kitchen window, Lyle has to scoot his chair over and draw the curtain. But this morning the cold air hangs still down in the meadow, and there is enough haze in the air to filter the sunlight so Lyle can lean on his elbows over a cup of steaming instant and smoke a Prince Albert and gaze out the picture window he now spends most of his life perched in like a hunched up old raven. The air, so heavy-cold and striated with strangely floating frost, is like cotton candy. Hoarfrost builds and grows on the fenceposts and pickets like tropical ferns, but white. White.

He looks out across the meadow filled with snow, across the leafless, oddly orange willow branches along the stream and on over to the wind-bared hill that heaves itself toward the evergreen ridges of the National Forest. The woodcutting trail climbs the bald hill: two parallel lines like railroad tracks, but where the hill steepens, the road curves around the worst part of the grade so that the foreshortened trail looks like a question mark hovering over the meadow.

"I've been staring at that confounded meadow and those idiot hills and lodgepole stands for over forty years now. I'm about done for and I'm still not sure I've ever *seen* any of it. All I know is I'm damned tired of looking at the sonofabitch."

He thinks about how completely the meadow changes with respective seasons, how much it can change under light and clouds between two times he raises his eyes from his book and looks over the top of his half-lens reading glasses.

When Lyle drives the Power Wagon to the top of the question mark and into the deep timber for firewood or to mow hay in the neck of the little side-draw, he can look back toward the house and outbuildings, and it always gives him a little start, as if he were looking into a mirror for the first time in a long time, like ten years, maybe. He can easily make out the old part of the house and all he himself added on. Then there's the barn he built in the winter of '74 just to more or less see if it could be done, the log garage and toolshed, chicken coop, root cellar, loading chute, corrals, garden fences, snowfences . . . A lot of damned fences, he thinks, like I was afraid I'd try to get away.

Hard to believe one man could get that much built from scratch in one measly lifetime. It's a lot different from what the family first found there: just that rotten barn sinking into the pasture like a ship going down, the old Worster barn at the head of the meadow, and the two-room home-stead cabin with its peaked roof like a witch's hat, now just a small part of the sprawling house he lives in alone. The old log walls, weather-darkened, covered on all sides but one with additions he built on.

Interesting, he thinks. A little sad. Possibly instructive. Funny how, when they first moved up to this place, there wasn't near enough room for all of them. Now the house was huge and with just him knocking around in all those rooms. All the others dead and gone.

While Henry was off in the Army Air Corps and Bob started building corrals and snowfences around them like a great exfoliating wooden rose, Lyle, then all of eighteen, fell to building the first of many log buildings he would carpenter from nearby trees. That was when the question mark began to appear above the meadow. It was a cabin for himself and Bob to stay in, and a shop where they could have a forge, some workbenches, and eventually, some real tools. He had built that cabin from the nearest trees he could find, skidding the logs with one of the half-dead horses they had. He drilled and pegged the logs together the old way because they couldn't afford spikes; only the roof boards and shingles had nails. But he found it a good way to build. Not as fast, but pegged walls are stronger than spiked, even if you could afford the spikes and the trips to town to get them.

So he stayed with the old methods and became a master builder with logs, increasing the size of the main house to a roomy and luxurious home with native pine paneling all hand-planed and tongue-and-grooved. Lyle began to develop a philosophy of technology that had to do with using whatever method did the best job, not like the rest of the culture he lived in, using the methods that were fastest. He used machines or worked by hand depending on quality. Time never entered into it.

Lyle and Bob built a big sawmill and went into business, not just milling lumber, but building houses, barns, and sheds for neighboring ranchers.

That's when Henry went down in the Pacific, and Bob, who didn't care for building and milling, got his own airplane and started crop dusting. His plane snagged on a powerline in Texas before he'd been at it a year. Then Clara started automatic writing and pretty soon she was hearing voices. The voices told her to take Lyle's rifle and put it in her mouth.

Hazel had always had problems with her legs hurting. They swelled into tree trunks, ankles wider than thighs. At age seventy-four the prairie-toughened matriarch finally died in the hospital in Laramie. She was the first member of the family ever to enter a hospital, and she was also, save one, the last.

Now there was too much empty space inside just like there was too much empty space outside. When the emphysema started to choke him the house got to be too much for him.

He stares out the window and thinks about how he first started to park the truck next to the front door instead of up in the shed because the short walk up the hill winded him so badly; how he began keeping split wood on the mud porch instead of out in the woodshed, beyond the snowdrift the lee of the house made; how he closed the door to the bathroom and shut off the pipes lest they burst. He went back to heating water in the kettle and bathing in a washtub the old way, standing by the woodstove's warmth. Finally, he moved his bed into the living room by the furnace, effectively moving back into the part of the house that was already there in 1940, before he ever built anything.

All the additions and improvements he'd made were useless to him. After all that work, he ended up back in the homestead cabin, all that progress for nothing.

But with his bed by the furnace he didn't have to wake with his own thin breath blooming above him like a sick rose. The whole process now was withdrawal, like a man freezing to death. The blood backs off from the fingers first, and the toes, and they go numb, then back from the ears and nose and face, then the legs and arms as the blood tries to get back to protect the heart, abandoning the five senses and any outward turning. Lyle turns from the window and rises to chunk another log into the fire.

If I'da knowed I'd end up like this, alone, I'da left things the way they was. God knows this old homestead cabin was plenty good enough for me." He sat down again at the window, placing a fresh cup of instant on the plastic-coated tablecloth that on one end had the pattern worn completely off from Lyle's elbows and on the other, where the company sat, looked brand-new.

He watched a young coyote descend from the heavy cover of timber and diagonal down the open hillside above the creek and disappear into the willows. "Better keep a move on today, Bud," he muttered, and turned his attention to the book that lay open before him: *Blacksmithing through the Ages*. But instead of reading he lifted his gaze again to find out what that punk coyote was up to. He could see nothing but the snow-stilled meadow with the coyote's tracks slicing down and across the hill.

His eyes stayed on those tracks, but somehow his mind lifted off and floated back to a certain spring four years after the family first wintered on Sheep Creek. Back then all they had was one Model-A pickup and the horses.

He was fording the creek down on the railroad section to go up into the timber for a load of posts when he saw them. It was a family of Japanese, fishing and having a picnic. They had a Dodge car that looked like it had fallen off a cliff. He remembered there were five of them. The teenage girl was the one he saw first, half reclining on the curved fender of the car. She was reading a pamphlet of some sort. As he drove down into the creekbed she didn't even look up, whether from concentration or fear he couldn't be sure. Then he saw an incredibly tiny and ancient-looking woman, he supposed the grandmother, who sat inside the car. She stared at him openly as he passed. She looked so frail and light-boned he thought a good wind could have drawn her out the window and up into the sky like a kite that's broken its tether.

The mother was down on her knees on the bank, blowing on a greenwood fire that was going to smoke the trout they presumed to catch. That's when the irony of it became more immediate in Lyle's mind than the images before his eyes.

Here were these people whose country had started a war against our country. Lyle's brother, Henry, was flying airplanes over families just like this one, bombing the hell out of them and whatever kind of tropical wickiups and paper houses those people lived in, and here was this family right up here on Sheep Creek, in the heart of the American wilderness, having an afternoon picnic.

"It's Henry as should be fishing and picnicking on our stream." Then he noticed the father, just upstream with a green willow pole, a can of worms, and a piece of kite string with a cork for a bobber, showing a small boy how to flip the worm into a deep pool and wait, keeping his eye on the cork. The man was gesticulating vigorously, pointing at the cork, and then throwing his arms skyward as if in surrender, imitating the setting of the hook, once the theoretical trout took the bait.

Even over the creek noise and the noise of the truck as it ground down against the gears and the compression of the motor into the gravel ford, Lyle could hear the man speaking in a singsong gibberish, high-pitched and rapid, that reminded him of a dry gate-hinge, or maybe a Western meadowlark, but off-key and arrhythmic.

When the man took notice of Lyle's truck, his face, at first awash in the happiness of a man who is proud of his young son and enjoying the role of father and teacher, turned like sudden weather, or more exactly, slid, like all the plaster sliding off a stucco wall in rain, into an expression of absolute terror. Lyle thought of crowds of faces just like that when they saw Henry's bomber, saw the American pilots coming in the sky, and they wanted to get out of the way but instead stood rooted, too terrified to move, with the fear that looks more like calm than calm does.

When the man recovered his wits he began poking the boy in the ribs and squealing a piercing, almost female-sounding command at him. Lyle tried not to stare but watched them politely out of the corner of his eye, the way a coyote would, and tried to watch where he was going, the rounded creek stones tending the skinny tires sideways as he entered the current.

After three or four pokes and attendant screeches the kid roused from his own paralysis, got the idea, and held up a tiny American flag he'd had all along, though lowered so that Lyle never saw it until it was held up for him to see. After another moment's hesitation the boy began to wave the flag in nervous and vigorous greeting. The father recovered a terrified grin and began bowing from the waist like a pump handle.

Utterly astonished, but impassive, Lyle slowly raised his big gloved hand from the oaken steering wheel and waved once, in the country manner. He watched relief flood the man's face like clear water turned into a muddy irrigation ditch. Then, in the mirror, he saw that the mother had turned to watch, but the girl and the grandmother had not moved. The little boy still waved the flag as the truck whined up the far bank and Lyle whispered, "I'll be."

He brought his load of posts back over the bridge two miles downstream to avoid the risk of getting stuck in the ford because of the extra weight.

Back at the house, Bob had not returned from the Wooden Shoe, where he had gone to trade eggs for milk. Lyle, his sister, and his mother were at the dinner table when the Japanese appeared again, this time lined up in a little platoon, single file, with the little boy holding the flag leading them through the yard gate. The boy was followed by his father. The ancient grandmother, who was about the same size as the boy, brought up the rear. Lyle saw them through the window, but he stayed where he was.

When Hazel heard the rap on the door she waddled over and opened it. Lyle, typically, had said nothing about seeing them before, and he watched as his mother stared, uncomprehending, from their faces down to the flag and back to their faces and down to the tightly clutched flag again. Lyle pushed back his chair and stood. Hazel was just plain stunned and wasn't hearing what the man said. She just kept looking from the man's face—his moving mouth, really—and down to the boy's flag as if they all were ghosts.

It was light but no sun yet. App lay under the wagon alone, staring at the undercarriage, the knotholes in the boards like eyes that looked back, the bolts, springs, brackets. He didn't know that some blood had dripped on his face as he slept. He saw some dried flecks on his right hand and thought nothing of it. He was cold and damp under the blanket, and dampness was something he had rarely experienced in these arid mountains. Oh, he had felt wet before, and cold, but he didn't know the mist that hangs in valley bottoms, the air like wet felt over the wet grass of the meadow. He could see his breath escaping like puffs of smoke from a train as it pulled out of the Union Pacific station in Laramie. He reached out his hand to the thick grass outside the relatively dry square: a rainshadow the wagon cast on the ground. App felt the heaviness of the wet grass and he liked it. On the Laramie side of the ridge it was like a desert compared to this. The icy Divide lay west; to the east over a series of ridges lay the high plains of Colorado that stretched in App's mind beyond thinking.

He rolled out from under the wagon and looked around, shivering. He could see individual droplets of water, lighter than the cold air, swirling in the first light that struck. The old man was nowhere to be seen. App looked down the valley over the cloud bank that lapped against the ridges and made them look like islands. He thought it looked like you could step off the ridges and onto the clouds and walk away into the sky.

When Frank got sick, I was just one of many who were grateful to help out. All the Lilley kids, all grown now, gathered around, of course, and Shirley, Frank's wife, started gathering her strength as if it were a crop of hay she needed to see her through a winter that was going to last the rest of her life.

Frank had a kind of cancer that no one gets over, which seemed to some of us altogether too meaningful about the world, since Frank was the healthiest, clean-livingest, most optimistic family man around. He didn't smoke or drink. He quit dipping snuff ten years ago. He'd spent his life on horseback, breathing in the Wyoming sky. But he'd been in the Navy during WW II, refitting ships, and asbestos finally caught up with him forty years later.

I wanted to help, even though I knew that so many others felt the same way I wouldn't have been missed. I asked Clay, Frank's son my age, to let me know what I could do. It was mid-October and Clay said I'd just as well help with gathering, vaccinating, and pregnancy testing.

It started snowing the night before the roundup. The horses in the corral were nervous because of the change in weather and being caught up well before daylight. I was on my way before first light, heading for the school section on my black mare.

It was cold. After I crossed the Sand Creek bridge the snow started going sideways and I had to get down and walk awhile to get the blood back into my feet. Clay had said to rendezvous around eight, which meant they'd probably have the herd gathered and headed home by then. Clay is always early the way other people are always late.

Sure enough, by the time I arrived at about seven I could

see the trailers already there and hear the whoops and whistles of the riders kicking the summerfat cows and calves out of the willows where they were lying-in because of the cold.

Every cowboy develops a whistle or a hoot or a click you can tell him by, a sound he thinks moves cows better than others. It's like a signature. I could hear Roger up in the corner, Clay down by the gate, and Shirley and Julie coming up the creekbed. By the time the cows were moving, like cold motor oil, all in the same direction, by the time they were through the gate and counted, the snow had stopped, the wind had died, the sun was getting hot. We drove them down the county road where it threads the picture rocks, those sandstone sculptures that were once an ocean floor, where we used to hunt arrowheads and occasionally lose ourselves when we were kids. Everyone was taking off coats and rolling up dusters to let in the warm sun.

We had a couple of pair missing so Clay and I broke off up a side-draw to look for them. I like to ride with Clay because he always rides a mount you don't have to wait for, and he doesn't like to wait for anyone else either. He doesn't mind riding in mutual silence, and he doesn't mind talking, as long as he doesn't have to crane his neck around to do it, and as long as it's "nothing too philosophical."

Dinner today is simple and mountainous: beefburgers, potato salad, and string beans on paper plates, beer and pop. Not a meal to linger over since there's a lot that has to get done before dark. We can hear the low moan of cows and calves finding each other in the corral. They are mothering up.

The first thing we do after dinner is separate the cows and calves, banishing the calves to the weaning corral. A couple of riders on stellar horses cut out the calves, and a couple of people stationed at gates open and close them when the time comes. The gates are like tongues catching flies, swallowing the calves into the weaning pen, clanging shut behind them. I like to work one of the gates so I can watch Clay and Roger work their horses, cutting with calm but quick predictive moves, their footwork like a boxer's.

Clay now works as a veterinarian out of Laramie, though he was raised right here on the Chimney Rock, and went to the one-room school at the Wooden Shoe (the other two pupils were his sisters). He backs the Bronco up to the branding chute and turns on the football game full blast, Wyoming vs. Wisconsin, loud enough to hear over the bereaved bawling of cows and calves, and begins to arrange syringes and bottles and needles on the tailgate.

Julie, Clay's younger sister, stays in the house with Frank, who shouldn't be left alone anymore. I can see Frank's face in the window. He is watching a ritual that, from the back of a horse, he has presided over every year for forty years.

Earlier, at dinner, when asked about some detail or other, Frank had said, "I can't worry about it anymore. It's up to you young fellas now," which made the young fellas, all in their thirties, ranch-hardened and some wearing the silver buckles they'd won at rodeos, feel like kids lost in a forest, the weight of their ignorance easily equal to the weight of Frank's wisdom, especially concerning a particular collection of sandstone, pasture, livestock, and weather known as the Chimney Rock Ranch.

Frank watches from the window all afternoon, with the game on inside the house. Once he walks feebly out to the corrals in the snowmobile boots he always wears now, even if it's warm and the ground is bare, because they are comfortable, and there are very few parts of his body left that are comfortable.

Shirley has to be outside with the pregnancy testing because she knows the calving history of all the cows better than anyone, and she has all the birth records and weights to decide which animals to keep and which to sell.

The hands had named one cow Shirley because she was born one February night of ten below when Shirley was out at the ranch alone during calving. There were complications and the mother died, but the calf was saved and grafted on to another cow. Shirley (the cow) went on to produce twelve fat calves for the herd in as many years. This year, though, she didn't take, was not vaccinated, and was sent through the gate that meant good-bye, despite everything. You don't get by being soft in this business. Shirley, the woman, just shook her head and penned an X next to the number corresponding to the cow's ear tag.

Roger and Brad are positioned on the corral side of the chute to dip the cows for parasites, trim the hair back from the ear tags, and check the eyes. I have a syringe in each hand, while Clay, who has donned coveralls and a shoulder-length latex glove, sticks his whole arm up the ass of each cow, feels around a couple of seconds and then screams over the screams of the herd and the football game either she's good or she isn't, and Shirley marks it down, and the hands at the gates know which gate to open when she comes out of the chute.

By now Clay's wife, Marrianne, has arrived with their

three kids, aged one, two, and three (Clay says they'll stop having kids as soon as they find out what's causing them), and some other neighboring ranch kids have showed up and are trying to help. Each cow is driven, prodded if necessary, down an alley toward the chute, which is opened like a loose jaw. When the cow sees daylight on the far side of the chute and tries to jump through, Roger throws the lever and catches the cow mid-air with a clang. Brad dowses them with an evil-smelling syrupy liquid, I stab each one twice when Clay gives the word, after his arm has withdrawn from the waterfall of fear-induced diarrhea, which by now covers not only his coveralls, but his pointy-toed, high-heeled galoshes as well.

The kids are running everywhere and shouting to Shirley all their questions about cows, as she writes things down on the clipboard in her lap. Marrianne is bottle-feeding Ely, little Oscar is screaming his head off about something. The football game is blaring, the men are shouting wry jokes and football commentary back and forth, the cows and calves are raising a deafening kind of rumbly howl. Laughter occasionally lifts above the din like a blue balloon. Frank is watching from the kitchen window, dying. I wonder what he and Julie are saying.

Lyle stood behind his mother. He was still chewing. The little boy was still clutching his flag. The man was trying to explain in elliptical but clear English that their car was mired and they needed help to pull it free. Without a word to his slackjawed mother, Lyle pushed her aside and started to walk up toward the truck, which he had already unloaded. The little family platoon followed him like goslings after the goose.

They all rode down to the stream again, the little boy on the hard bench seat next to Lyle. Lyle could feel the boy's skinny thigh pressed against his own as they bounced along. The father and the girl rode in back. Out of the corner of his eye Lyle could see that the blue paint was worn off the stick where the boy was made continuously to clutch in his moist little fist the symbol that was the literal and only defense his family had in this dry, limitless foreign land. I bet he goes to sleep hanging on to that, thought Lyle, as he stopped the truck behind the family's car and let it idle.

Lyle could see that the car's wheels had cut deeply into the sod and that the axle was resting on the grass. Lyle knew his pickup did not have the weight and traction to pull the car out, nor would a draft horse be able to budge it, but he had to give it a try to prove it to the father.

Just as he had foreseen, the rear wheels spun, frivolously as a fortune wheel at the county fair, and had no more effect than to slick the grass down. The car humped a mite each time Lyle pulled, but it wasn't coming out, and the drive wheels of Lyle's truck were beginning to cut their own slots in the sponge, so he gave it up and offered to drive the family back to town. They'd have to wait for the bog to dry.

Lyle could imagine the effect on his mother of boarding an entire family of Japanese overnight. So without stopping at the house to explain, he drove them and all their gear into Laramie.

It turned out they ran a small restaurant in Laramie, a place Lyle had seen and wondered about but had never been inside since he and his family did not permit themselves the luxury of eating houses. The Japanese father, who now rode in the cab with Lyle and the little boy, extended profuse invitations to Lyle all the way to town. Lyle, the man said, could eat at the restaurant free anytime he wanted for the rest of his life. So grateful was the man, he never stopped bobbing his thanks. He also explained that they, like many Japanese-Americans in Wyoming, were not sent to camps because they were citizens of a landscape in which the government could not imagine them doing any harm. The townspeople were generally tolerant of them, sympathetic, even giving them enough business to keep going. But his family was afraid all the time, the man explained, and occasionally people said cruel or threatening things to them. Lyle just kept glancing sideways at the little boy and his flag, and then back to the blood red dust of the county road. He steered the truck like a PT boat flying colors on the bow all the way across the oceanic basin into town.

Lyle considered this memory of his a mere curiosity, an anecdote with no apparent content, an interesting occurrence. It was the kind of thing the mind returns to in its freer moments, as before sleep or at the end of life. It was, to him, a circumstance to which he had responded the way any ordinary, decent person would have responded, but it was strange, a little magical. He never did go into that restaurant to eat for free.

Still staring out the window Lyle pokes all of his hand that will fit into his shirt pocket. He fishes out the cigarette papers and Prince Albert tin he has cut the bottom off of, shortened to fit shirt pockets, and soldered the base back on. Anyone who has tried to fit a full-sized P.A. tin into his shirt pocket knows they are built the wrong size, so you can't quite snap the pocket flap over it. Every time you stoop to pick something up the tin falls out, plopping into the spring, for instance.

Lyle's fingers are enormous, whether from heredity or hard work or both, I couldn't say. His hands are like bunches of bananas. It's quite something to watch him separate a single leaf from a book of papers, hold it between three fingers, fill and roll a smoke, and lick it shut. He hangs the cigarette from his lower lip and sweeps whatever loose flakes have leaked out the ends off the table and back into the tin. He drops the tin back into his shirt pocket and snaps the flap over it. From the other breast pocket he uses the same two-fingered technique to extract his Zippo, which produces a flame about six inches high. He flips it open and strikes the wheel with the whole palm of his hand. Though he tips his head sideways, his eyelashes are all singed off from lighting cigarettes. He needs a good-sized flame to light his smokes in the wind.

This ritual accomplished, he turns again to stare across the meadow. He wonders where that coyote pup has got to, what he's spending so much time doing down by the creek. Trying to ambush the mink whose tracks Lyle saw yesterday, or just wasting time sniffing around a beaver house?

This is the second dream. I'm coming home after a long absence and for some reason I take the Cherokee Park Road up from Fort Collins. I stop off to see how Lyle is and he seems not just better, but not sick at all and about ten years younger. We sit at the kitchen table and look out over the meadow, which is just about ready for cutting, and drink coffee like we always used to. Lyle doesn't mention any news.

I say so long and start to drive up over the ridge for home and am horrified to discover a huge construction project under way between my place and Lyle's. They are moving a lot of rock and gravel around, and when I ask them what they are doing they say they are building a dam, another reservoir. But they are building it in a place where there is no stream, no water at all, and they aren't using any modern machinery. They are using horses and mules pulling wagons and slips, and there are a lot of them but they aren't making noise and they are tearing things up something awful.

They have also broken the cattleguard across my fence. I start screaming at them and threatening them and they seem terrified, but they don't stop working. They apologize. They say they have orders. They keep working. They are dressed in clothes from the last century.

Then Clay drives up in his pickup and says he doesn't think it's time to do anything yet, but if I need him to help me stop these men, even if it means shooting them, if they don't just quit pretty soon, to let him know and he will help me.

I say I don't know about shooting them because I think they might be Amish or something, but I will if they keep building this lake between me and Lyle, and Clay says they can't build a lake because there isn't any water. I say if they finish the dam and there *is* water we will have to shoot them even if they are Amish. Clay says okay and places his hand on my forehead, which is not something he would ever do. The hand leaves a burning red mark. Then he gets in his truck and drives away. I can see my house from where I am and it looks okay.

Those first years on Sheep Creek things were harder. Lyle had only one auger bit, and as for drill bits, a lot of little holes got filed into bigger holes because he lacked the proper sizes. He had one old crosscut saw, half of whose rake teeth were missing, and whose cutting teeth had been filed so often their tops were where their bottoms used to be. Lyle's family had no running water, no electricity, and two rooms and a lean-to for the whole family. Still, their spirits were higher then, even if they were less comfortable and more afraid.

Clara and Lyle had read all about Holland, where all their forbears were from, and they asked Hazel a lot of questions since Hazel had spent her girlhood in a town in Iowa that was almost all Dutch.

Clara got it under her bonnet that they should have some winter fun skating on the beaver ponds the way Hollanders skated on their canals. "I wonder if a body could skate away, down the Poudre to Collins," she said. Lyle just snorted, but when she took the money from her last summer's painting and sent away to Monkey Ward's for four pairs of the kind of skate you adjust and bind with leather straps to an ordinary pair of high-topped shoes, they all were excited.

The skates appeared in the big mailbox that everyone shared for packages which stood beside the row of ordinary boxes down at the Wooden Shoe Ranch. Lyle brought them home one day coming back from town.

The next morning was sunny, and they all snowshoed across the meadow, skates slung by the straps over their shoulders, to the biggest beaver pond on the creek. It wasn't exactly like the pictures in Clara's books about Holland, what with the beaver house out in the middle of the pond, but the ice was thick and the wind had scoured most of the snow from its surface. Lyle brought a broom to tidy up their little rink.

The ice was rough and Lyle remembered how they laughed that day, each of them trying to stand and go a bit, and the bubbly laughter that ensued each time their legs flew out and they landed with a crack on the unforgiving ice, skated feet stuck straight up in the air. Their bottoms were mighty sore after that first day, but not as sore as their stomach muscles from laughing so much. That was the last of the skating for everyone except Clara and Lyle, who took to practicing every day for a while, until they could loop gracefully around the pond together, holding hands and swinging themselves around each other, skating in tandem, arm in arm.

Lyle flicks the long ash from his cigarette. He watches from the kitchen window as his dead sister and his younger self glide elegantly and happily around their own private skating rink in that meadow tucked back in the mountains, where no one else could ever know or see, with all the happiness they ever held inside themselves at one time, when the family was far too poor to be fooling around with exotic sports. But Lyle was twenty and Clara was alive, and poverty seemed the least of burdens a man could hold in his heart.

Now Lyle catches sight of the young coyote angling back up the bare hill toward the edge of the evergreens where the ridge begins. The coyote is drenched and his usually apparent bushiness has collapsed around the reality of his impossibly skinny frame. He is carrying something in his mouth, even more drenched and limp-looking than he is, something that he carefully drops in the snow long enough to look back over his shoulder at the house, where smoke rises from the chimney into the sky without a twist or curl, so straight it looks solid.

He licks his left forepaw, probably cut on the ice. Lyle wonders if the coyote can actually see him, the only other animal around, where he sits in the kitchen window. Lyle often wonders how well different animals hear or see or smell, and what, for instance, it would be like to see what the red tail sees, to be behind his eyes, or to smell mice under the snow asleep, the way coyotes do. To *see* with your sense of smell would be to see things narratively, to know not only where things are but where they have been, and how long they have been gone, as if everything seen had a gently diminishing streak behind it like a comet, showing where it came from and how fast it had traveled. To hear what an owl hears, a mouse rustling dry leaves a hundred feet down in the timber, in a tangle of roots and undergrowth.

Lyle knows that coyote isn't much concerned about being followed or hunted, since he's passed by here so often before. Lyle thinks it's more a matter of showing off, showing Lyle, who had doubted the wisdom of hunting the creek bottom on a day as cold as today, that it had indeed paid off, and that he didn't mind being soaked to the skin in ten below. So he turns and fixes his gaze on the kitchen window in a superior kind of way, then picks up the brown lump that is now rolled in snow like a drumstick in flour, and haughtily trots toward the cover of the timber.

Lyle stubs his smoke and says, "Better keep movin', you little bastard. It's cold and your ass is soaked. You fell through the ice and got drenched just to catch some goddamn disgusting muskrat that you are going to eat raw while you shiver yourself dry, and you think that's something to be proud of. Well here's to you, you puffed up little bastard. You can have it. You're a fool to survive if that's all your life is for. But I'll say one thing for you. You're tougher than a pine knot, by God. There's no denying you are one tough little hombre."

As soon as the sun found the valley, it warmed and the mist rose straight up. By the time the old man returned with an armload of wood to boil his coffee on the sun felt hot. App thought the meadow was like a nest, ringed by ridges and sentinel pines. Sheep Creek lazed in its deep willow cover. App figured it would be an easy matter to catch a nice brook trout for breakfast if the old man would give him time. Warming himself in high-altitude sun he studied the anomalous lushness around him. Just beyond the ridge lay the dry, rocky slopes he was used to, the sagey emptiness of home.

"It rains a light rain here when it isn't raining anywhere else around, then the sun shines. Rain at night, sun by day. It should do that everywhere. Why it doesn't, I guess I'll have to ask the Devil," he said to himself.

He spread the damp blanket to dry on the gray dome of a boulder that stuck up out of the meadow like a bullet. Steam rose from the blanket and it reminded him of winter, standing next to the woodstove, soaked through, steam from his shoulders wreathing his ears.

As the old man got the fire lit App limped through the tall grass. It soaked his ripped trousers from the knees down, wet as if he'd waded the creek. He thought if the old man was paying attention he'd think App was just going to take a piss or get a drink from the creek. As long as he didn't ask, App might get a little fishing in before the water boiled.

When he reached the bank he squatted down in the tall brome and almost disappeared. He studied the water. The quicksilver glimpses and their shadows flashed in and out of the shadow of a rock in the middle of the current. He stood quickly and leapt out on the flat surface of the boulder and flattened himself, belly down on it. His sudden shadow over the water had dispersed the trout like grass blades thrown into a gale. He waited happily as the sun warmed him and he rolled up one sleeve. Soon the trout began to trail back, lazily toying with the currents the way hawks and ravens play with updrafts and breezes. He began, almost imperceptibly, to lower his forearm into the water. He watched his arm as he reached, making sure its descent was slow enough to be taken for stillness, like the hour hand on the old man's pocket watch that App liked to stare at, trying to decide if he could see it move or not. Of course he couldn't move his own arm that slowly, but that's what he was trying for.

When his arm was fully extended he moved his hand underneath the rock, still slow in the current, until he touched a fin slowly wavering like a gently fanning angel's wing. In his mind he could see the beautifully speckled body as he moved his hand forward to the slick cold under the gills. He began to wave his hand gently from the wrist like a willow branch trailing the current. He stroked back along the sleek form toward the vent to see how big a fish he was rocking to sleep. It was fourteen inches or so, big for a native brookie, enough for a good breakfast.

He massaged softly, working his hand forward, and when his hand was behind the gills again he knew the fish was dead asleep. In one swift motion he grasped it and lifted it out of the water in a shower of gemlike drops that fell back into the creek, which was itself as full of light as it was of water. With a deft motion of his left hand he shoved the head up and back until he heard a definitive snap. He leapt back to the bank, his hand already reaching into his pocket for his clasp knife.

One cut, slick as a zipper, from vent to gills, revealed the inner mysteries. The second cut popped out a flap under the chin. He inserted his thumb and pulled, removing the lower fins, gills, and viscera. He threw them all in one piece back into the stream. It made a gulping sound where it went under. He slid his thumbnail down the bloodline in the spine, dunked the fish, closed his knife one-handed against his hip, and emerged from the willows, breakfast in hand.

The trout had gone from living to cleaned in thirty seconds. One minute later it was turning on a willow spit, and the coffee water was beginning to boil. App looked into his father's face that stared greedily at the fish and decided to feel happy anyway.

As the horses leaned into their harnesses and the wagon scraped and groaned toward the top of the ridge north of the valley, App could see how the valley pinched off to almost nothing between rock outcrops and then opened out again just upstream. He could feel the air getting warmer by increments as they climbed out of the valley. It struck him as decidedly female. It was too high for cottonwoods, but there were willows and aspens, and the hayfields fanned out on either side of the narrow granite waist. The valley made an eight. The hills all around were covered with dark green lodgepole stands; the aspens were splashes of lighter green among the pines and in tributary draws. App was trying to count how many different greens there were dancing in the early light down in that hidden valley. It reminded him of a walled garden, like he'd heard of in foreign cities, though it was surely as untrammeled as any piece of ground in the inhabited world. He was happy just to have seen it and spent one night down in its cool lushness.

App was still turned around looking when the old man stopped in front of the team and the horses slowed, too, and stopped. They had reached the ridgetop and the old man was letting the horses blow. App could see the whole Medicine Bow Range winding around to the northeast like the tail of a lazy cat, and the Snowy Range shown above it like clouds that had turned to salt and could never move again from where they hovered above the blue ranges.

Opening to the right was the Laramie Basin, vast and dusty, reddish and choked with sage, its far end undefined except for the pale blue mirage of Laramie Peak, a broken piece of sky that had fallen like a triangular shard of mirror.

Everything ahead was open—red, brown, and blue. The prairie's mother was unresisted wind that worked all winter to keep her child's ears and elbows clean—an amount of scrubbing no tree could survive. App twisted back around on the bench again to see the manifold green of the valley one more time. The wooly morning air was still steaming out of it in places. App thought, *I want that.* He said nothing but turned forward again, the vision still behind his eyes as the wagon lurched forward and he felt the sun on his shoulders again.

Once it's all over Clay and I lead our horses through the gloaming to stable and feed them. I'll leave my mare here and catch a ride home in the pickup. We walk up to the house for our coats as the night air starts to sink into the valleys.

I stand by the coal stove waiting while Frank and Clay speak in low tones in the next room where Frank lies on the couch breathing oxygen. They are talking about how many cows are pregnant, how many cows and calves they will ship, how many are blind in one eye or otherwise afflicted.

I'm standing there hearing their voices, but I can't hear the words exactly. I smell the coal smell of the heater. The armchair is buried under a drift of overcoats, dusters, and slickers. The huge elk rack on the wall (I think it was Clay's first) is massed under cowboy hats, both felt and straw, some for work, some for wearing to town, and plaid winter caps called Scotch caps of every description and hue, some of them blinding, as though somebody killed a mess of ugly couches and made hats out of them.

In the corner on the floor is a mountain of footwear, mostly Frank's, though now he wears only those spongy moon boots. That pile of boots has been in that corner as long as I can remember: cowboy boots curled up like croissants, dry and cracked or polished for town; boots with spurs and boots without spurs; boots inside cowboy boot galoshes; booted galoshes with spurs, booted galoshes without; shoepacks for feeding in winter; work boots for summer—all in a heap about three feet deep.

I hear the drone of the cows and calves moaning for each other, and the low chiaroscuro tones of Frank and Clay talking in the next room.

Next morning Clay is cutting the herd by seven and the cattle begin to bawl. I'm working the gate on one end of the scales, and after each calf is weighed and I turn it out I yell something like "Steer X19" or "Heifer Y4," and Clay, who is reading the scales, shouts the weights, and Shirley writes it all down, occasionally yelling, "What?" over the din. The ground is still frozen but the sun is hot.

Brad swings a portable gate behind me, this way or that, when Shirley decides which calves are keepers and which are going to be shipped.

When we are just about done I see Frank's small, wiry frame emerge from the house and begin its inimitable, bow-legged, ducklike walk across the yard in those moon boots and an old black felt hat. Nobody ever walked like Frank that I ever saw, though I've seen a lot of guys walk like they are not used to being off a horse.

Frank comes up next to me. Until recently he was as curly-headed and stout as one of these grass-fat steers, but now his hair is gone from treatments—all but a few strands. What's left has grayed. He has aged about thirty years in three months.

He lifts one of the snowmobile boots up to rest it on the bottom rail of the corral and sticks his arms out over the top rail so that it's kind of hanging him by the armpits. His hands are clasped inside the corral and he is quiet for a long moment, looking over his herd.

Then he says, "You know, that horse of yours wouldn't be worth a damn to anyone else." A long pause while he lets that sink in. "But you've got a lot of patience." Pause. "You're bringing her along pretty nice. Stay with her and someday she might even be useful. I was watching you from the house." Another long pause. He jabs toward the mountains with his chin. "You know, there wasn't enough snow up there last winter to melt down for a cup of coffee. I thought surely the pasture would burn up by the end of June. But I'll be damned if it didn't rain just about every so often, like this was some kind of sensible country to live in. The grass this summer was the greenest I've ever seen all my life up here. And you look at those calves now. Fattest we've ever raised. And the percent of cows that took is higher, too. Now what do you make of that?" He turns to look at me for the next long pause, but he doesn't really expect me to answer. He knows I'm just listening.

"Here I am pussyfootin' around with all my hair falling out and the country looks like damned Ireland or something." Pause. "If it don't beat all. 'Course I don't blame anyone. The Navy didn't know about asbestos in 1946. I'm glad that the one who got sick was me. I'm just glad it wasn't Shirley or one of the kids. I couldn't'ta stood that." Long pause.

"Asbestos is just one of the things we come up with to make this a better world, and ever so often one of those things goes haywire and some poor sucker like me pays the price. But I sure don't blame anyone. You can't blame the whole damn Navy. Or civilization. The world *is* better now than it was when I was your age, and me and Shirley started out at the Running Water, cooking on the woodstove and trying to nail down the livestock so it wouldn't blow away. My Lord, it's windy up there. Things are a lot better now, though I know you and Clay don't think so. You weren't there, now, were you?" He turns to look at me again, expecting no answer.

"You know, that Clay—him and Brad and them put up hay faster this year than I've ever seen anybody put up hay. Like the Devil was after 'em. And for once I didn't have to worry about a thing, not broken balers or thunderstorms or any of it. I just sat back and watched it get done. Best year of my life.

"So green.

"Not to mention all my kids havin' kids faster'n I can count. Greenest year I've known, bar none. Now I'm goin' down the road before you all bring the herd. I'll be ahead of you guys and have the gate open when you get there.

"And don't forget to take a load of hay home with you for your horses. This hay we put up this year is almost as good as what Lyle used to make."

Frank turns and duck-walks over to the Bronco. The rest of us saddle up and take the herd that's staying on for winter. We have a little trouble at first when we turn them out of the corral and they want to go every direction, but we sprint our nags and whoop till they start down the road, bawling all the way like they're sad the summer is over.

Frank stops the Bronco on the hill until he sees we have them moving, then he eases down the road. We chouse them the two miles down to Oscar's meadow (the Wooden Shoe), where Frank is waiting by the open gate. We count them through and Roger has to rope one calf and yank him into Brad's trailer. Somehow that calf wasn't supposed to be here.

Frank closes the gate behind us, and we slowly start back up the road for home. It is just getting dark. I twist around in the saddle and watch Frank watching us ride away. He takes off the black felt Stetson and, holding the brim curled, lifts it once into the air.

School had started, but not for the Worster boys. It had been a summery October and the first snow had fainted away so fast it was like the perfume of a passing girl. It occurred to Raymond that the episodes of his life all faded that fast. There were parts of his life so ephemeral that they didn't even qualify as stories, more like dreams already woken from. Like his father's first wife, who was beautiful, they said, but weaker than the year's first snow, who died before she ever got a chance to be Ray's mother. And the ranch, too, the ranch on Sheep Creek that App mortgaged to pay the doctors and lost. And Ray's own mother, App's first wife's sister, who died bringing Jack into the world. Now he was wondering if anything at all lasted, anything you could grab on to before it slipped past, beyond blame, beyond meaning.

Ray had missed so much school already it would have been better, from his point of view, to go ahead and miss the rest of it. It had become humiliating. He was almost too big to fit into the desks. He liked the teacher, Miss Gunnerson, though, and the schoolhouse at Tie Siding was warm and had pine floors, not dirt like home.

App always pulled the boys out of school when it was fine enough to work. Here it was October and they hadn't even been yet. Ray was beginning to think of himself as a stupid person who would make his way in life by the sweat of his brow and the strength of his back, which at twelve was already considerable.

Ray watched App tuck his flowing white beard inside his shirt so it wouldn't get caught in the grindstone. App pumped the treadle and let the wheel throw drops of water in the shape of a galaxy as it spun. He sharpened the eight blades of four axes for the morning's work.

When App told the boys stories of his early life, they seemed like just that: stories. It seemed to Ray as though none of it had really happened, though he knew all of it was true: how green the meadow was, how much hay it made some years, how much stock his father had to feed in winter. How the cabin had floors, like the schoolhouse, and no one had to fetch water because the water flowed from a spring above the house, through wooden pipes that App had drilled out of lodgepoles, right up to a tank by the front door. It didn't freeze in winter either because the pipe was buried deep and the water was always running so no one had to melt chipped ice or snow to drink. How there was a woman in that house who was their mother. How App had lost it all.

Ray wondered where things like that went when they were gone, and, even that young, he longed to go there.

Ray looked around at the claim shack they lived in. Hell, they didn't even own the dirt floor under it, let alone the walls and roof. They weren't trying to prove up any claim— App knew the ground was worthless. They all knew it was a matter of time until they lost the shack, too.

Every morning App sharpened the axes and they drove the flatbed up along Boulder Ridge, sometimes all the way into Colorado, almost as far as that meadow that was supposed to have been their home, their own land to work and build on.

Things seemed to have a way of going haywire, as if there were some other kind of gravity in the world that pulled things in the wrong direction: Someone else got the homeplace and they lost two mothers.

Every day Ray and his brothers scoured the forest for cured pitch pine. They cut and split the logs they found into fenceposts; they shouldered the posts out to the road and loaded them on the old Chev. App hauled them to town where a supply store paid him fifty cents apiece for posts that, once set in the ground, would not rot in a man's life-time.

But the good cured pitch was getting harder and harder to find, and Ray noticed he was spending more time wandering through the woods looking. He didn't like looking. It was just more time to think about how he'd already lost everything before he ever got a grip on any of it. He didn't like the direction things kept pulling in and he didn't like thinking about it. Swinging his axe, working up a sweat was about the only time he gave those thoughts a break, outside of sleeping.

App handed the razor-edged axes to the boys and they rode the back of the truck up the sharp spine of Boulder Ridge on the road that had been made by the railroad tie hacks when they put the Union Pacific through. You can still find the worn-out ox shoes they tossed by the side of the road.

The boys were silent before the day's labor. They would stop for half an hour at lunchtime (which they called dinner, though it wasn't even much of a snack), and then go back to work until it was too dark to see. Maybe one of the boys would see a bear, or pick up an arrowhead, or lay his boot open with his axe without scratching his foot, something to mark the day somehow, to set it apart so that memory could find it, but usually the days were the same. Anonymous. By the time they got home, had eaten their supper and turned in ("Time to scratch the feathers and purr," App always said), there wasn't much dark left before it started all over again.

It was four-thirty. Ray had just carried three posts out of the timber to a side trail and was walking back to Nigger Bob Creek. He still had a good hour of work to do before App called them in. He was scanning the forest floor for pitch logs when he saw something that was, to him, more rare and strange than any ox shoe or Indian knife, something so foreign to his twelve-year-old mind that he did not know what to do.

He saw a human being. A man. A man fishing. The man had a peg leg and was wearing a buffalo coat, but neither the leg nor the coat made as much of an impression on Ray as the simple fact of a human in a place where Ray had never seen anyone who was not his father or his brothers. It was the first time Ray had ever seen anyone he didn't know.

The stranger was standing on a beaver dam with his back turned. Ray let his axe drop and tiptoed up behind a big balsam fir to watch. He was mesmerized. He watched the man from behind the tree until it was so dark he was afraid of not being able to find his way back to the road. He was afraid his father and brothers would go home without him. He turned and fled, quietly as he could, forgetting the axe where he'd dropped it, for which App gave him the thrashing of his life that night.

They found the axe the next day. Fifty years later, Ray said, "You think you've had to adjust. I was twelve years old before I ever saw a stranger."

With half a bottle of rum in his hand, Ray made a lateral sweeping gesture, like he was using the jug to brush a fly off the table, only there wasn't any table. "They ought to e-rase the human race and put something good on here. When I get down to hell I've got a few questions for that Devil, real sticklers, like how come they let people into this world when it would have been perfect without them. I mean if you imagine the natural world without the human race, you are thinking of something perfect, perfectly balanced, that just keeps going. Only thing as messes it up is the people. Especially when they try to *manage* things. The more of 'em there are the worster it gets. Now how come they done that? That's going to be the first question. After that there's the long list and the short list, depending on if he's got time, which I imagine he's got aplenty of, but you never know if he takes questions or not."

Ray took a healthy pull and wiped his mouth on his sleeve and passed the half-gallon of booze. Some fisherman had given it to him as a bribe to fish in the reservoir where the company didn't allow it. The news that the Chimney Rock Ranch had sold its Colorado holdings had reached us, which was why we were parked by the side of the road up to Deadman, blind drunk, taking turns weeping from rage and grief.

Not that it was anything new for the big ranch that, along with the National Forest, surrounded all of us to be selling land. Frank Lilley had been foreman down there for thirty-five years, but the multimillion-dollar spread kept changing owners, usually among Eastern wheeler-dealers looking for places to hide their money, or big corporations like Western Union—six times that I could remember. Frank had always stayed on, though he had no assurance of keeping his job from year to year. The ranch stayed a cattle operation; it just shrank from 90,000 to 72,000 acres and increased in value from one to six million dollars. We were crying because this time they had sold six sections in Colorado to Colorado land developers, which meant the summer cabin, hunting, fishing, and recreational vehicle set was moving in. The land we'd roamed free all our lives was about to be sawed up and nailed down into forty acre "parcels" all the way to Wyoming, the whole foreground of our view. About a hundred low-budget refugees in Winnebagos and fly-away shacks were massing for the invasion since the land was being pedaled at bargain basement prices. Most of the plots had no trees or water. People would be told it was a good investment as well as a recreational paradise. Only those of minimal intelligence and maximal faith in realtors' lies would fall for it. Many of them would throw away their life savings.

Ray said, "Jim, I never saw a stranger till I was twelve years old, but I've seen a passel of 'em since. You got to realize it's going to go that way. You got to cry a little more and take it. There's no way in hell to stop it. Oh, you might put a crimp in their get-along, but you can't stop 'em. And it ain't nobody's fault, neither."

Ray put the truck in gear and drove a hundred yards down the road, not bothering to shift into third. He pulled over again, cut the motor, and took another pull from the jug. "Yessirree Bob, Jim. You've got to realize. And so do I. You own a whole section, and these people that are fixing to ruin this country just want their own personal little piece of heaven. We gotta move over and let 'em in. You've got your section. You've got your memories of the used-to-be same as I do, and they can't squat on that."

"Ray, there are so many of them they'll make a trailer court out of the wilderness they are after. It'll be a country club for white trash. They're going to eat it up before they ever have it, and we won't have it anymore either. Those jackasses actually believe it when the realtors tell them they'll be able to get in here all winter and the creeks run high all summer and that the price of land will rise forever. They are going to build ugly things down there where we've been looking at nothing so long we're addicted to it. We won't be able to see the mountains for the junk they are going to strew down there."

Then I told Ray the third dream. "I'd been gone awhile and when I came home there was a ski lift on the old logging trail my dad calls the Champs Elysees and the prairie was all paved over and they had parking spaces on top for people to gawk at the view from up there.

"You know how sometimes things happen in life so bad you wish it was a dream but you can't make it a dream so you can't wake up from it no matter how much like a bad dream it is? In this dream I had that feeling. I knew it was real and I wanted it to be a dream, but I couldn't make it one, even though this time it *was* one. I even reached down and touched the warm dirt where they'd bulldozed it off to the side. There was sagebrush and prairie flowers and grass mixed up in the gravel, and they had scraped it right to the bedrock.

"I reached down and touched the gravel and flowers to try to wake myself up by not feeling it there. But it was there and there were these guys in slick Western suits and alligator boots. They had blueprints rolled up in their hands and then I was screaming at them that they had made a mistake, they didn't own this section. 'Hell,' I said, 'you don't own any of it, but even by your rules you don't own this. By your rules I own it. You have no right to destroy this ground.'

"At first I couldn't even get them to look at me so I walked up to this one bastard and screamed right in his face.

90

He said they had surveyed it all, and if I'd lived there my whole life thinking it was mine I'd been living in the wrong place. The Caterpillar diesel started to crescendo and drown him out like surf. I couldn't hear him, but then I somehow convinced him he'd made a terrible mistake. He looked around at the ruined hillside that now resembled a strip mine. He said it wasn't his fault. It wasn't anybody's fault, and besides, what good would it do if they stopped now?

"Then I was pulling out my grandfather's service automatic, the one he used in the Philippines, the one we shoot old horses with, and I'm raising the barrel into his face, and even though I don't want to shoot him anymore I know I'm going to shoot him anyway. So I'm pulling on the trigger, but I don't hear it go off because the bulldozer is so loud, and it's just this guy's terrified face floating up into the sky like a sunset right there in the middle of the day."

I took a swig to keep from crying. Not that I minded crying in front of Ray, but I thought if I started crying now I'd never be able to stop.

"The first thing I noticed was something white and shiny on one of the bare ridges west of the abandoned Running Water Ranch. It was like a snowdrift that begun to appear in July and kind of spread out across the hillside. You could see more of it from the county road coming back from town than you could see up close because it disappeared behind the scrubby hills. Evidently it was spreading northward from the summit of the ridge, since, from the south, you couldn't see nothing but rabbit brush and blue sky.

"Frank knew what it was from the start. I figured it was one of the new parcel owners doing something, but I couldn't figure what. Anymore, even to go down and look was trespassing. So I just wondered—and figured some day to know—what was making the north side of that ridge go all white and glittery in the middle of summer.

"One morning I had just sat down at the kitchen table when I heard a pickup howling by in compound low. It was one of them trucks with a backseat, and it was pulling a four-horse trailer, and behind that there was another little box trailer made from the bed and rear axle of an older, junked pickup with round fenders, like maybe a '56 F-100.

"That's when I put it together.

"The trailers were overfilled with junk, mostly old appliances—washers, dryers, refrigerators, freezers—all mixed in with more nondescript pieces of white enameled sheet metal—shower stalls, possibly—and auto body parts.

"This man was bringing his Kentucky bank account from whatever hovel or digs he inhabited, probably on the north side of Fort Collins, or maybe La Porte, up to his new country estate, which was a treeless, waterless ridgetop that would be a sure-enough wind tunnel in three month's time, at least five miles from the nearest source of electricity that

92

could power any of those appliances even if they could have been fixed or used someday.

"Clearly this yahoo intended to *live* up there, in the style to which he was accustomed, on forty acres of exactly nothing, and he was moving his security blanket first. God help us.

"I begun to witness daily trips. The man's big wife would drive the junkmetal wagon train down to Fort Collins (sixty miles, mostly dirt road) every morning, where she apparently held some kind of steady job at the livestock auction. His kid stayed mostly in town; the old man himself stayed mostly up on his piece of prairie. The truck bed and trailers were full of firewood cut to length for sale on the trip down, which was a curiosity since this man had no timber anywhere near his property excepting the National Forest, which I figured he figured was as much his as anybody's. When the truck-train returned at dusk it was always full— a new load of broken refrigerators and shower stalls.

"I took some interest in this operation, which went on for weeks. The white, shining junkpile begun to spread across the hillside so that if the sun was westering you could see it glint all the way to Laramie, thirty miles.

"Also, the man, whose name I learned from Frank was Earl Ferris, was a marvel of sleepless energy. At the same time he was pilfering wood to sell in town and hauling trash up here, he built a rickety, battery-powered, two-wire electric fence with plastic ribbons all around his forty; *and* he was building a flat-roofed frame appendage to his fifties-model Airstream trailer that he lived in. Not to mention that he was noted poaching at night and trapping on some of his neighbors' parcels—those few, that is, who were lucky enough to have a drainage and enough willow bushes to make a beaver dam. I figured he must have thought he was here a hundred years ago, and a beaver pelt brought fifty dollars instead of fifteen."

Ray once showed me a map of the original homeplace on Sheep Creek his father had had drawn. It was a plan to build a dam where the rock outcrops pinch off the two parts of the valley like a girl's waist. App intended to sacrifice the upper meadow to save the rest. He wanted to get financial backing in Fort Collins to build a reservoir. He planned to sell water to the dryland farmers in eastern Colorado. Irrigation had just started coming into the country. App was a very smart man. He was right on time.

The map showed topographic contours, where the dam should go, and how much water it would hold. App had paid a right smart to have that map surveyed and drawn. Floating on the imaginary lake were the words *WORSTER RESERVOIR*. It was supposed to pay off the doctors and set him up for the rest of his life. It was his retirement plan. Somehow things got pulled in a different direction.

There's a lake there today but it isn't called *WORSTER RESERVOIR*. It's called *EATON*, and it didn't save App's land. And that high-altitude puddle isn't the only thing in Colorado that bears Eaton's name, either. There's a town and banks and schools and libraries and God knows whatall else. Just like the great railroad builder Ivinson, in Laramie, who charged his Chinese and Irish laborers 40 percent of their paychecks just to cash them, and had everything in town named after him.

When Mark Eaton got wind of App's plan, he leaned on the backers and got them to withdraw. Then he waited until App was desperate. He bought the upper meadow from App for a pittance and built the reservoir himself.

Ray said it would have been all right with App if he hadn't gotten rich off the only scheme he ever schemed, but it wouldn't have cost those moneymen a cent to name the reservoir after the man whose idea it was. But life's ironic, and blame won't stick to anyone: App's last straw turned out to be the best thing that ever happened to Ray sixty years later.

After swamping for ranches at a dollar a day for years, living in bug-infested bunkhouses, Ray followed the lure of city lights as country boys have always done and always will do—that gape-mouthed awe for the electric unknown pulls them in like moths, or else it's just wages, pure and simple.

After Ray married Margie, a hometown girl whose father owned a plastering business and considered her to have married down, they moved to Denver where Ray got a job welding. The war was on and what Ray welded was airplane wings.

Since the Army wouldn't let him fight (he never told me why), he decided to give more blood than a whole platoon of soldiers. This, combined with the effects of welding indoors, poisoned him to where the doctors gave him two weeks to live. Margie drove him back to Laramie to die, but he recovered in six months' time and hired on with Margie's father as a hod carrier.

Old Roy always hated Ray, but no one could say that the son-in-law was afraid of work, so Ray learned the trade, and because Old Roy wanted what was best for his daughter, he eventually bit the bullet and made Ray foreman.

By the time Old Roy was ready to retire no one wanted stucco anymore. Sheetrock was coming in, replacing lath and plaster. But Ray didn't have another trade—outside of welding, which his health denied him—and there weren't enough pitchpine posts left in the woods to surround a gopher hole.

So Ray bought the business from Roy, and the business slowly died. As much as anything else, it died because Ray couldn't bring himself to charge any more than slightly less than what would have been fair, especially to anyone he knew, and he knew everyone in town. Furthermore, by the time he was fifty, he had begun to drink up a considerable percentage of the profits and had started missing payments on the doublewide.

In 1972 the irony showed itself. Ray received a call from a man who said he was a water engineer for the Divide Ditch and Water Company, which owned and operated Eaton Reservoir. Ray's reputation for his knowledge of the back country—where the company had miles of ditches which fed, along with Sheep Creek, Eaton Reservoir—had come to the man's attention. Bill McMurray, who had run the ditches since 1948, was retiring, and the man wanted to know if Ray wanted his job. It would mean less money, but the company would pay all his expenses, give him a house to live in just below the dam (I always thought the house was situated to insure that the caretaker took care of the water flow properly), and a new pickup every four years. The man also said the company was buying a snow vehicle, like a lightweight Caterpillar, so he wouldn't have to snow-shoe or snowmobile the nine miles up to Deadman, as Bill had to do all these years.

Ray was interested. He sold the plastering business for a neighborly price, paid off the doublewide, and moved up on the mountain.

He still didn't own the house he lived in, but he was living on his father's homeplace, his father's dream, which was now half-drowned and half-owned by some fellow named Lyle Van Waning.

So Ray became a water engineer, my neighbor, and Lyle's, and Frank's, and began to roam the Deadman country, running the ditches, cranking the headgates, rebuilding some of the things Bill McMurray had let slip into ruin, and generally keeping an eye on things. One of the big pluses was that there wasn't much to the job a man couldn't do drunk, and the boss was sixty miles away.

Out of habit Ray fixed everything with cement and chicken wire, like retaining walls and crumbling foundations. What he couldn't fix with cement he welded. He hated to build with wood, hated driving nails. He would rather build a fence of welded pipe than wooden rails, and he liked the idea of things lasting.

Ray was home at last, by God, and he reckoned he couldn't die now since he was already in heaven. Every time he thought of his good fortune, he just had to drink to it.

It's just a pitchfork with the handle sawn off and the tines forged over to ninety degrees, a specialized tool for pulling mud and willow sticks from culverts and irrigation ditches. Lyle sits hunched over on the tailgate. His hip boots are turned down. He flops the handle of his ditch tool back and forth from hand to hand between his knees. He smells mint growing in the willow bushes along the creek, listens to the even cadences of Ray's treatise on the Supreme Intelligence of Beavers. Lyle is not all that receptive to Ray's point of view.

"A beaver can construct a sturdy enough dam to stanch near any mountain torrent. He likes a reservoir. He doesn't need a backhoe or dynamite. Now that's a water engineer. He isolates his house, out in the middle with the door underwater so he won't be bothered."

Lyle interrupts. "Maybe I should have built my door underwater."

"You should have. That beaver has perfect security. He's warm all winter and has plenty of supplies. Going to town for him is as far as the nearest aspen tree."

"That's usually where the coyotes catch them." Lyle stops flip-flopping the handle and looks hard at Ray. Ray pretends not to notice and keeps talking.

"When the pond freezes to his liking he goes down to the dam to pull out a few sticks, like turning the crank on the reservoir, and lets out a little water. He lowers the level to make an airspace and room to swim around in there. He does it before the ice is too thick so he can't get trapped inside. It's just like that'ere Holidome in Collins. In summer that water is so still, it works just like a burglar alarm."

Lyle listens. He knows all this, but that doesn't make it any less interesting. It isn't what people say, he thinks; how they say it is what really tells you what they're talking about. His sour mood is not the result of disagreeing—in fact, quite the opposite. Lyle hates it when Ray says things he agrees with.

"Sure they're smart, Ray, but that don't mean I have to like the sonsofbitches. Being smart just makes it worse. Makes them better at being a pain in the ass. Makes you feel guilty for trapping them. Hell, Ray, *people* are *smart*."

The inkling of a smile begins to play around the corners of Ray's mouth. He is about to experience the sublime joy of getting Lyle's goat.

"I suppose you'd feel that way about coyotes if you was a sheep herder. Why they're smart is why they're a aggravation."

"Number one, I ain't a sheep herder, and number two, I'll tell you who's a aggravation."

Now Ray just beams. He covers his grin with his hand to hide the teeth he's missing. They stop talking.

Lyle thinks about how good beavers are for the meadow since they raise the level of the creek and slow the water down so it has time to seep into the sub-soil. When they plug the ditches, though, they mess up everything. Lyle doesn't like being forced to trap them. Last summer he tried to trap a beaver near the flume with the usual shoulder-hold Victors that drown them, but, expert as he was, he could not. Some beavers, like coyotes, cannot be fooled. One morning he found a trap sprung and there was a toenail in its jaws. Lyle knew enough not to be encouraged by this. It meant that beaver would be even more careful, at least for a while.

Lyle then hooked up a twelve-volt battery to a wire he strung across the pond about an inch above the surface. When he came back next morning more or less expecting to find a beaver floating dead on its back with smoke still coming out of its ears, instead he found that the beaver had raised the water a notch and shorted out the wire.

That beaver must have been impressed with Lyle's ingenuity, though: it moved upstream and started to rankle Ray. It plugged the culvert under the road that leads to Ray's house. The water rose and washed out the road. Ray was calm. He didn't want to drown a beaver cruelly in the usual trapper's manner, so he went down there four nights running with a bottle, a flashlight, and a shotgun. He never saw anything. He needed some sleep. The next morning the culvert was plugged and the road had a chasm four feet deep running across it. Ray was cut off. And pissed off.

He built an elaborate scarecrow and dressed it in clothes he wore all the time, for musk value. That worked one night, then the beaver got wise and sawed off the road again. Ray waited in ambush another four nights and didn't see anything. He parked his truck down there, which worked one more night. Only. Ray was devoting his life to this beaver.

He broke down and set traps near the places he could see where the beaver slipped in and out of the water, leaving little muddy slides in the bank's sweet grass.

One morning I went over to have coffee with Ray and I found his truck parked down by the culvert. Ray was slumping on the tailgate like he was passed out from booze but hadn't fallen over yet, but it was too early in the morning for that, even for Ray. I walked up and there was the biggest female beaver I have ever seen laid out drowned in the back of the truck.

Ray didn't look up. He said, "There's a whole mountain back there with streams and springs to plug no end. If I could've scared her, but she wouldn't scare." When he looked at me his tears made freshets down his cheeks. We walked to the house for coffee before skinning her out.

Though both of his brothers died flying, Lyle told me he didn't have anything against airplanes except they were too "vibrational." Ray had welded fighter wings, but he never went up in a plane. Dr. Bert Honea had a very used bush plane. It wasn't fast, but it could climb like a nighthawk and it could land on less than half a mile of tundra.

Bert took a notion to land his winged rattlebox on the two ruts and hump of grass referred to as "the road." When he came in for his initial landing he buzzed the house first. I tore off down the hill in the Jeep, with a rag tied to a stick of lodgepole for a windsock, and parked off to the side of the runway.

Bert flew over twice more to test the wind, which, as usual, was every which way, shifting from side to side like a cat twitching its tail to mesmerize a sparrow. Bert decided to forget about the wind, since it had no apprehensible direction, and land the thing uphill so it would stop faster, he hoped, before it reached the fence or a lick of crosswind swiped it into a spin.

On his final approach he was wobbly. I could see his jaw muscles bunching, and his knuckles were white as sugar cubes when he clattered past me at eye level. He hit the road surprisingly smoothly, taxied up to the top of the rise, spun her around, and shut the motor down. The age of flight arrived on Boulder Ridge in the summer of 1981.

It ended that same summer when Bert came down a little harder than he meant to and the landing gear collapsed. Lyle came over and figured out a way to brace things up again with some light chain and a come-along. Bert didn't like the looks of it so we all set to work unbolting the wings. Lyle was horrified to find each wing secured by only two bolts.

"Two bolts? Two bolts, Bert?" The plane went out on the back of Lyle's 1930 REO.

For a while Bert was landing and taking off on that road as if it was routine. One Saturday Bert offered rides to everyone, so they could see the country from above. Everyone came but Lyle. We took turns going up in the two-seater. We saw what loggers had done to Deadman. We saw the sand rocks like a batch of meringues. We saw our own houses.

Ray had been hanging back. "Oh, no, you go ahead. I ain't in no hurry." I wondered if he was afraid to go up, but when I thought about it, thought about Ray, I knew that wasn't it.

Bert said, "Ray, you're last. Now or never."

Ray got ready to speak by covering his mouth with his hand. He pretended he was feeling his beard, but really he was hiding his bad teeth. He said, "Bert, I've spent my whole life on this mountain, and I just don't think I can stand to see it look small."

One of the things modern medicine has managed to do besides turning hospitals into churches and doctors into priests, is to infect the culture with the foreknowledge of distantly imminent death, something human beings don't really have it in them to cope with. What I mean is, we are supposed to live knowing we are going to die; we are not supposed to live knowing when.

The modern victim of Intensive Care often goes from someone who knows he is going to die, at some unpredictable time, to someone who is in danger of imminent death, to someone who doesn't have a chance and knows it. I'm not talking about the time it takes for your life to flash before you. The body ticks on horribly, without hope. And everybody has to know about it, too, especially relatives who are forced to talk more about miracles than is dignified.

Bert Honea told me that when he was a resident in an inner city hospital he had to learn, for the most part, to divide the patient's complaints by ten to get an accurate sense of the degree of pain and the seriousness of the condition. When he moved to Laramie and set up his practice, he learned that with ranchers you have to take the complaint and multiply by ten to know where you are.

Example: A guy about ten miles west of here, cutting poles in the National Forest, broke some part of the drive train on his truck once it was loaded. He jacked it up and went to try to fix it. It fell off the blocks and crushed his legs.

Luckily there was a CB radio in the cab that he could reach and he raised a neighbor lady, and what he said was, "Hello, Ruby? How ya doin'? Say, is Don busy?" By the time they found him he had passed out, but they managed to save his legs.

Another example: A young woman whose husband had died, but who stayed on at the ranch alone was robbed one night by two strangers. They shot her twice in the face and threw her body in the root cellar. Two days later she crawled out and drove herself to town.

In old age the same woman, still living on the ranch alone, got a call from friends in town who couldn't get out of their driveway because of a heavy snowfall. Louise drove her Jeep twenty miles at night through the blizzard, pulled them out of the driveway, turned around and went home. She got stuck herself about a mile from her house. While digging herself out, the Jeep, which she'd forgotten to leave in gear, rolled over her leg and broke it. She crawled home and went to bed. When her leg still hurt in the morning she called the doctor.

Anyone who knew him would have thought Frank Lilley was far more likely to get blasted out of the saddle on his hundredth birthday by a bolt of lightning than to go down the way he did.

So when Frank came into the clinic to see Bert, the very fact was worrisome to say the least. For about four months Frank had had a pain when he breathed or lifted his arm. He said, "It doesn't really hurt or nothin', Bert, it's just that something's not quite right in there."

Bert started out hoping for curables, but Frank went from being someone who is going to die someday to being some-one who is as good as dead, and everybody including him had to know about it and go on living with that knowledge for months.

The day I saw Roger come out with his horse trailer to move the herd from the Sand Creek pasture was the day I knew Frank was done for. I don't know how I knew, ex-actly; I just watched that plume of dust burning down the county road like a fuse and I knew.

The Civic Auditorium was the biggest room they could

find for the service. They say it's a terrible thing to see a grown man cry, but when you see a whole roomful of tough-as-jerky, dried-up old cowpokes who never talk except to say hello, good-bye, and excuse me, all broken down with weeping it's kind of a relief. That day in the auditorium there were a lot of very tough people, men and women, choked up.

Arlo Hewlett, the county extension agent, had to stop in the middle of his eulogy, which was mostly a story about how the county commissioners (of whom Frank was one) took Frank to a seafood restaurant and tried to get him to order fish. Frank said, "Boys, to me, seafood is a cow standing in the stock pond." Arlo had to stop in the middle and say, "Excuse me, ladies and gentlemen, I've got a kind of a catch in my throat." He stepped back from the microphone and stood stone-still for about two full minutes before he went on with another funny story.

Other people stood to speak. The preacher talked about Jesus, but was honest enough to allow that, though Frank took Christ as his saviour, he was no "Religionist" and never went to church, but worked on Sundays like any other rancher any other day. He never needed any church but the one he rode over on his horse.

After the audience filed out I sat as the pallbearers loaded the flag-draped coffin into the hearse, and then the room was empty except for Frank's old saddle up on the stage, an old, burnt-up lariat coiled loosely and hung over the high, old-fashioned pommel and saddle horn. All around it were flowers.

Ray never wanted any funeral, but after they got the body back and thawed it out and zipped up his pants, Margie, his new widow, took over. She loved Ray, but she wasn't going to let an opportunity like this slip by.

First she sent word that she wanted me to come to the funeral with my guitar and play some of the old Western tunes Ray loved enough to play all night. When I tried to say I couldn't play in front of a lot of people she said it would be just family: Ginny, Lainie, Bill, Jack, and a few kids. The same people Ray and I used to play for every Saturday night at my dad's house.

It's hard to tell a grieving widow no, especially one whose hairtrigger tears soak a litany of hankies. Once she found a hummingbird dead from whacking into a window. She built a little mausoleum for it out of white quartz pebbles and pine needles. Ray kept expecting it to smell but it never did. She used to bring it out and cry and show the thing around to company. You see what I was up against.

I told Margie I'd play, but Bert had to play, too. The morning of the service I drove into town to Bert's house to put on a suit. He showed me the morning paper announcing the funeral at Striker's and inviting the whole town. Bert and I were mentioned as musicians.

I must have looked like I'd been kicked by a horse. "I thought Ray didn't want a funeral service."

Bert said, "He didn't, but Ray's dead."

I said, "How can Margie do this?"

Bert said, "She ain't dead."

At the bottom of the announcement it said donations were being accepted by the widow for a headstone. I said, "What headstone?" .

I called up Margie and she cried and cried and I couldn't get anywhere. She said Ray would be cremated next day and he'd wanted to be spread out on Boulder Ridge from the tree with the rock stuck through its trunk all the way up to Deadman, but she couldn't face it yet. I said, "What about this headstone?"

She said she was behind a couple of car payments, Ray's drinking cost so much at the end, and without Ray to provide anymore, and no workman's compensation, she didn't know what to do. Maybe some of those old friends whose houses Ray had stuccoed for free would repay the favor now. I hung up, and said, "What do we do now, Bert?"

Bert said, "Bite the bullet."

So we took our guitars over to Striker's and they gave us a little room to sit in that was out of sight of all but a few people on the edge of the audience. The man in charge of the home said all we had to do was play one song while people filed in and one song while they filed out, which didn't sound too bad.

I could see Harris Ankeny in the audience. Harris plastered with Ray for twenty years. After he fell off the scaffold and wrecked his legs he worked as a janitor at the University. Harris used to come up to the ridge with Ray, especially in winter on snowmobiles, not just because he liked it, but to keep Ray from getting too drunk and getting into trouble. I know he thought if he'd been with Ray that last time it would have turned out different. Harris sat there like a stone statue in the rain.

The funeral director gave us the nod and we started to play "Red River Valley." After we'd played it all the way through they were still filing in so we sang it. Then we played it through again but they were still filing in and we stopped. The funeral director glared urgently at us and made a motion with his hand like he was cranking the starter on an old car. We started to play another song.

We must have played ten songs, everything we could think of for a funeral. When we played "Rio Colorado," Ray's niece, who was born with something wrong with her brain, set off keening like a wounded bobcat and couldn't stop. It was a spooky sound.

The preacher got up and said some stuff about Jesus and how Ray was in heaven and hadn't really died at all. I knew Ray thought heaven would be a step down from Boulder Ridge, and I thought about his questions for the Devil. Then it was over and everyone started out and we started pumping up songs again, some of which we hadn't played in years.

I've been to visit Margie since and she never changes. She watches "soapies" and fills up the doublewide with crocheted knickknacks, whatnots, and bric-a-brac. For instance, she made a little sombrero and a serape for her bottle of Tabasco sauce. I ask her when she wants to go up on the ridge to scatter Ray's ashes. She still isn't ready; they're under her bed. She got about $300 toward the headstone, though, so she still has something to drive. God bless her.

LYLE, 1981

"The first time I come face to face with Ferris was on a Sunday afternoon and I was taking a snooze after dinner. I woke with a start, though I didn't hear anything, and there he was peering through the screen door at me where I was lying on the couch. He'd come up on the house afoot and was just standing at the open door looking at me through the screen, which is one thing, I guess, in town, but out here it's very damned strange. It gave me the willies and I jumped up off the couch and said, 'What do you want? Jesus Christ.'

" 'Howdy, good neighbor,' says the voice behind the screen. 'Sorry to be botherin' you, but my truck quit me back down the road a piece and I was wonderin' if you had some jumper cables you could borrow me a minute to get her goin' again.'

" 'Sure,' I say, because around here you just don't leave people stranded. I still didn't like being sneaked up on, though, and I still couldn't make out the stranger's face through the dark screen backlit by a bright afternoon sun. Then I started to wake up a bit and I asked, 'You mean it was running and it quit?' He nodded. 'Then a jump start won't help you. Cables are for starting cars that won't start, not for starting cars that won't run. If it quit you something else is wrong. Where is it?' He said about halfway between here and Ray's. The way he used Ray's first name surprised me. It was like he'd known him for years.

" 'If I can just get it up over the hill I know I can get it home. I own some land up here, you know,' he said importantly.

"By then I'm awake enough for it to hit me who I'm talking to and I say, 'Well, if you think it will do you any good I can loan you some cables. But what are you going to jump it off of?'

"Then, unbelievably, deadpan, he says, 'Can I borrow that 'ere truck?' He jerks his chin in the direction of my Studebaker. My heart slid down to about knee high as I thought of the nearest phone seven miles away, the nearest wrecker thirty-five miles away, and how once I got involved with this outfit, I'd be responsible for their well-being. I couldn't refuse them. You just don't do that. I also wasn't about to loan this stranger my truck and have him hitch it up for the locomotive to his junk train.

"So I put on my hat and stepped out into the yard and was immediately startled by the presence of another man, a younger man, standing about fifteen feet off to the side, out of sight near the window.

"Once outside I could see the face of the man I'd been talking to and I didn't like what I saw. He was gray-haired and handsome-ish, tall, with squinty blue eyes—like he was staring into a bright light all the time. There was something else about him, too, that kind of chilled me, a slackness in desperation, like a deer whose throat you are about to cut. His skin was the color of brick cement, heavy on the lime. He was unshaved, but not bearded. He looked like he hadn't bathed for a year or more and there were clots of black greasy muck in his ears tufted with hair. His clothes were so filthy with grease and dust, their original colors were hard to make out. It was like someone had dipped him in used crankcase oil and rolled him in the dust like a chicken-fried steak.

"The younger man, clearly his son, was pretty clean by comparison, black-haired, but with the same squinty blue eyes like I was shining a spotlight at him or caught him in the headlights as he was doing something illegal. I decided not to think about it.

"The three of us climb into the cab of my truck and head up the road. When his truck come into sight I despaired another notch. It had quit on a steep incline, right in the middle of the road. Hooked up behind it was the usual massive load, but instead of junk metal it was livestock. There was three horses in the trailer, two goats in the cart behind it, and crates of chickens in the bed of the pickup. Now I was really in over my head in terms of responsibility.

"What if the truck wouldn't start, as I suspicioned it wouldn't? What was I going to do with these people, and worse, what was I going to do with the animals? Where was this greasemonkey going to overhaul his truck? If he had no booster cables, did he have any tools at all? Money for parts?

"Then I caught sight of the most chilling vision of all. Sitting stock-still in the backseat was the hulking form of an enormous woman, possibly the ugliest woman I ever seen in my life. She had a pronounced moustache and her eyebrows were a straight thick line like a piece of greasy rope stuck to her forehead. Her hair was curly black and all sprangled out, and she had on this tiny straw cowboy hat that looked like she must have screwed it on. The look in her eyes said, 'If you address one word to me I'll tear your head off and suck out your guts.'

"Ferris was looking at me with those eyes, squinting, disaster-accepting, a depending-on-the-kindness-of-strangers denial of responsibility for whatever happened next.

"I pull my truck up bumper to bumper with his and we raise the hoods and connect the cables. I jump into my truck with unreasonable hope and fire it up. I gun the motor and shout for Ferris to give it a try. Ferris says nothing. Ferris does nothing. Ferris squints at me. Finally he looks up at me and says, 'It's not ready yet.'

"He sat inert in the driver's seat of his vehicle, and he wouldn't turn it over. I yelled for him to start it, but he just smiled and said it wasn't ready, at which point I understood that his battery was indeed dead, his generator shot, that he knew it perfectly well, and that he intended not to jump start his truck, but to charge his battery off of mine at the risk of melting not only the cables, but the wiring in both vehicles.

" 'Start it!' I said, and when he still wouldn't I jumped out of my truck and headed for his to do it myself, mad enough to forget about the enormous, evil-looking wife in the backseat. Ferris waited until I was reaching for his door before he pretended to turn the ignition and quickly turned it off again for a few more amps.

"I stood in front of his open truck door. 'Why don't you let *me* try it?'

"He says, 'Okay, okay, okay, here we go now,' and then he waited a few more seconds. He turned the key and it started.

"Without the generator working and with so little charge in the battery, which was running the truck by itself—which Ferris knew when he left Fort Collins—I knew I wasn't necessarily out of the woods yet, though luckily nothing in the electrical system of my truck had been damaged. If they made it over the top of the ridge, it was downhill all the way to the junkheap, which was apparently now going to be a barnyard menagerie as well.

"I said, 'Get the hell out of here while you've still got some battery.' He nodded pleasantly and squinted at me. Even the ugly woman gives me a tiny squeak of a smile. She had been sitting there, still as a sphinx, stalled out in the backseat for a couple of hours at least, with the goats and horses and chickens in crates threatening to expire from heat stroke.

"Ferris put it in gear and began to grind his fantastic contraption up the grade toward the ridgetop. I made several deals with God before he made it. I had fallen in behind as the caboose of the unlikely train pulled by the little engine that I hoped to Christ could, and when we topped the ridge and the Ferris train begun to pick up speed on the downward grade I was sure relieved.

"Ferris gives me a jaunty wave out of his window, and I'm left with the gray aftertaste of knowing that these people live less than four miles away. In fact I could *see* the top of their junkheap with binoculars from the ridge.

"For the grace of God and the deals I made with Him, I personally never spoke to Ferris again, though I seen him from time to time, and his wife, who continued the daily pilgrimages to whatever kind of steamy heap they lived in formerly, and they still brought the daily bargeloads up the mountain, having fixed their brutalized pickup. But instead of junk it was always livestock after I helped them out that day, until there was twenty or more horses of chaotic variety, half as many goats, innumerable chickens, ducks, geese, and even peacocks, not to mention the manifold dogs, cats, and whatever that family had living in their clothes. It wasn't long after the arrival of these folk that Ed Wilkes was horrified to catch in a trap set for packrats in his cellar the only honest-to-God city rat that has ever been seen on Boulder Ridge."

W hen they surveyed the state line between Colorado and Wyoming it didn't come out right. Both states are almost four hundred miles square so it wasn't much of a surprise to the surveyors when they ended up with a fifty-foot discrepancy. They never fought over it because it wasn't an overlap—they both came up short.

According to Colorado that ribbon of land fifty feet wide and four hundred miles long was in Wyoming. According to Wyoming it was in Colorado. According to App Worster it belonged to him since nobody else wanted it. He'd lost the meadow on Sheep Creek and figured he could build a claim shack on that strip and neither state would require him to prove up, which would be helpful since he knew there was nothing under the state line but rotten granite. App guessed right. Even after the second survey, which came out right, neither state seemed willing to notice which side of the line App's house really was on. He lived there thirty years, to the end.

When he nailed the last shingle on the roof, whose ridgepole ran east-west, he stood up there and spread his arms out wide and tilted back his head and shouted at the sky, "Mine!" and laughed and cried at the same time. Then he said out loud to himself, "Sure hope I never have to fence the bastard in."

Both Ray and Jack were born in that claim shack. App still hoped to get the ranch back, but when his second wife died he gave it up. He gave up a lot of things then— everything but waiting. He shipped off his three sons by rail to the state of Washington to live with his dead wives' other sister (the one of three he hadn't married). But one year later they arrived back at the station in Laramie, each with a bulk freight tag around his neck. Three tags that read: *App Worster, Laramie, Wyoming.*

Many ranchers were building vast mileages of fence in those days, so there was no lack of work cutting fenceposts on Boulder Ridge. Before long App bought a flatbed to haul posts, and a car, a Model-A, to drive to town. When the ridge was too snowed in to work, he let the boys drive the car to school at Tie Siding.

The country between the claim shack and the school was open prairie. After a big storm it blew into drifts and clear spots. Neighbors gave the boys permission to take down fencewires if they had to when meandering among drifts looking for a way through.

Driving across a prairie in winter, it doesn't matter where the road is. You keep to high ground, exposed to the wind. You puzzle your way, sometimes backtracking, sometimes digging through. You try not to think of yourself from an aerial view.

The Worster boys always had a lot of fun driving to school. The Model-A was a good car in snow, far better than its modern equivalent. Its wheels were thin enough to cut down through the snow and reach the frozen ground for traction, and it had a lot of clearance under the differential. The boys raised rooster tails wheeling among the drifts; they turned the gearbox around so that all the car could do forward was howl along at a walking pace. They drove across the prairie at twenty or thirty miles an hour in reverse.

One winter App's leg started to swell for no reason anyone could tell until it was big around as a gatepost and just
as stiff. The boys convinced a doctor to come out from town
to look at the old man, since App said he was damned if
he'd go crawling and complaining to some upper-level veterinarian who would just want to saw the thing off anyway,
which is exactly what the doctor proposed to do. He said
the leg would kill App if he didn't let him. App told him to
go to hell.

"Open the door, Ray, and let some of that sunshine in
here. I don't know what's wrong with this damned thing,
but I know a little sunshine will cure it." App spent all spring
and summer sitting in the open doorway, chewing Day's
Work plug tobacco, which he hardly remembered to spit
out, just more or less ate, and bathing his leg in sunshine
until it started to shrink and he could walk. By fall he was
up on the mountain again, driving the truck and saying over
and over, "Let that be a lesson to you."

August of 1955 Ray took a Saturday off and hauled the
whole family up to Snowy Range for a picnic and some
fishing. They went in the old log truck because there were
about fifteen of them with all the kids and in-laws. App
wouldn't eat and went back to the truck and just sat in the
cab. He stayed there all afternoon, until Ray got worried.

"You all right, Dad?"

"Sure, fine. The strangest thing, though . . ." App was
staring hard into the deep, clear, glacial lake below the white
stone and snow of the faces. "I felt kind of peaked so I came
in here to sit awhile and I saw Marie. I saw her like I see
you sitting there now. She said she had been waiting for me
all this time and that everything would be all right. We just

set here for the longest time holding hands and chatting about this and that and not to worry about the boys. But she was still young and her hand was so young here in my old one . . ."

App died in his sleep one week later and was buried on Boulder Ridge where the ground is so hard Ray and Jack and Pete had to use dynamite and drills to get the grave deep enough. They worked for two nights and days with tears streaming down their faces, staying drunk the whole time. When they were done they put App in a number two pine box and buried him. Ray took the bar and pried up a good-sized boulder nearby for a headstone. With a hammer and cold chisel Pete carved in the stone a letter A, then a P, then another P, and called it good.

When I was seven Clara died. When I was seven nothing seemed strange. When I was seven *so this is how it is* is what I thought about whatever happened. Clara didn't seem "off" to me. Everyone said incomprehensible things. She was nice to us kids, took us arrowhead hunting in the picture rocks and at Bull Mountain Spring. She laughed and was a little homely.

Clara said that Indians walked placing one foot exactly in front of the other, instead of a little off to the side the way we walk. She gave us a demonstration in a pair of beaded moccasins she'd made, being careful, also, as she said, to put the toe down first instead of the heel to make less noise. She said she wanted to make less noise and also to leave more beautiful tracks in the snow. She was going to practice until she always walked that way.

She studied occult texts. She became a Rosicrucian. All winter she talked to herself and painted landscapes. Often she depicted animals—deer or elk or horses—looking up as if they'd just heard something, some danger, but hadn't seen it yet.

She was trying to live too far away, seeing few people and rarely going to town. The wind blew the winter long. She kept painting the vistas that shut her in, surrounded her with their fatally indifferent beauty. Icy landscapes covered the walls. It was like not having walls. She practiced automatic writing every day and contacted voices. The voices started telling her to do things. Lyle came over and asked my father if he would try to talk some sense into her. "When I talk to her she's just yonder."

My father went and Clara was talking out of her head, like she was from someplace far away and wanted to get back. My father said they had to take her to the hospital

118

right away. Hazel insisted that they could calm her down and keep a close eye on her and that they'd go in tomorrow—it was already late. They'd go tomorrow.

Lyle never drives faster than a crawl. Sometimes when he drives by on his way to town you don't hear him, the way he babies the engine. That's why I remember how he tore up our drive later that evening, wheels throwing gravel into the air like sprays of water. His face looked drained, without surprise or any possibility of surprise. I'd never seen his face like that before. It made me cold. Lyle was standing on the porch talking into the darkness behind the screen. "You can't do nothin' for her now, but maybe you can do something for Mom."

After an hour or so my father came back in Lyle's truck with Lyle and Hazel. My sister and I had been put to bed. Lyle and Hazel sat in the living room with my mother. My father drove to Fort Collins to get the coroner. My sister and I lay on our cots listening. It was dark in our room and there was a bar of light under the door. The grown-ups' voices sounded urgent and weary. They were talking about how Clara had seemed suddenly better, lucid again. She'd become cheerful and was singing happily to herself as she took her sketch pad and said she was going into the sun for a while. The next thing, they heard the shot.

When my father got there she was still breathing, but not for long. When he arrived in Fort Collins the coroner asked him why he hadn't brought the body with him. He (the coroner) wasn't going all the way up there at this time of night. So my father headed home to get an old rug my grandmother had braided, then over to Van Waning's, where he wrapped the body in the rug, then back to Collins.

We were all having breakfast and no one was talking. My father drove up and came in and got some buckets and rags and a mop and went out again. As he left, he hung my grandmother's rug, which now had a dark stain like rust on it, over the back fence next to the forge.

Octber 1963, Thursday. No one around for miles. Lyle is building a new room on the homesteader's cabin we live in. He's been hard at it since eight this morning and now it's past six. He didn't go home at noon today. He wanted to finish the rafters so he just brought a sandwich and a thermos of coffee.

Hazel's bread rose so aggressively the slices looked like cross-sections of a huge mushroom. The same damned slices that had embarrassed him at school. Good, though. The sandwich was elk meat that Bill McMurray had shot two falls ago and Hazel had canned. By noon the coffee in the steel thermos was just warm.

Lyle had spent the day cutting out and laying up rafters, first figuring the angles for the pattern so the rafters fit flush against the ridgepole and the notches in the rafters fit the plate on top of the wall, which in this case was the top log itself, hewn flat on the outside and with notches chiseled in the top to make right angles. The rafters themselves were roughsawn two-by-sixes that Lyle had milled on his sawmill.

You have to keep your tools sharp. You have to be willing to spend half an hour every so often to sharpen your saw, your chisel, your axe. If you keep your tools sharp and aren't afraid to move your arms, power tools are unnecessary. If you keep your tools sharp it isn't that much slower to do it by hand, and the results are better.

Lyle lifts another rafter onto the sawhorses, lays the pattern on it, and marks it out. First he crosscuts, then he rips. The ripsaw sails through the wood. His arm strokes steadily till each outcut drops.

Electricity, he thinks, is overrated. Hazel, and Clara before she died, had urged him to put in a power plant for lights and a water pump so they could hook up the water jacket on the cookstove and run water through the firebox and back to an insulated tank and have hot water from the faucet, like people do in town. Lyle went along because he wanted electricity in his shop. He'd had some ideas for power tools he wanted to build, starting with a metal lathe.

He got a junked Windcharger from the Diamondtail Ranch and rebuilt it. He traded for a bank of thirty-two-volt deep-cycle batteries. He'd set up the house for lights and it had been nothing but headaches ever since. The batteries eventually wore down and had to be replaced. Lightbulbs blew and were increasingly hard to find in thirty-two volts. The wind was often still or raging like a banshee. He couldn't leave the charger on if he was away from home.

Having electricity started giving the women ideas: an indoor bathroom, a phonograph, and then it just snowballed.

He liked having the power tools he'd designed himself and made from scraps—two lathes, three drill presses, a table saw, joiner, planer, lapidary saw, grinder—but unless you were setting up for a really big job, most things were just as easy to do by hand, if you knew what you were doing and kept the tools sharp.

Lyle hoists the rafter to his shoulder and climbs the ladder with it and sets it in place, driving in one tenpenny nail to hold it. He climbs back down and sits on a sawhorse. He fishes out his tobacco. As he lights up, the sun is setting, turning the sky as many pastels as you see on the side of a rainbow trout. The reddest clouds are the fish cut open. Aspen trees are peaking with yellow. A wind comes up the draw, announced in advance by clapping aspen leaves, and then he can hear it take the pines around the house and he feels it on his cheek and it makes the end of his cigarette glow brighter. He takes a deep drag and looks down past the springhouse nested in orange willow branches. Up over the opposing hill he sees the snow on mountains west of Laramie. Another breath of wind comes up and starts the aspens chattering like nervous girls, and they catch the last low-angling rays of sun and flare. The dark tops of evergreens are red, almost bloody, and for a good thirty seconds he knows that the world is something altogether other than what it appears to be.

By the time he puts his tools away and starts the Studebaker down the drive it is full dark. He can see the light brown gravel of the road where it contrasts the gray-green sage and blond grass and he drives home without turning the headlights on.

By welding a Model-T axle and a bar of tool steel to either end of an arm's length of pipe, Pat Sudeck made a bar for chipping out postholes in rock, the kind of bar Lyle calls an idiot stick. It's heavy enough for its own weight to do some of the work, and the pick and blade are so hard you have to draw them out on the forge to sharpen them. After it's heated and hammered out it is crucial to temper it right or it will either crumple (too soft) or break (too hard) when it strikes a piece of granite.

Tempering different grades of steel is a subtle art that can't be explained in any book. People see colors differently, so that the relationships of colors as they shade down a metal rainbow from red to purple to tan, can only be hinted at. It takes years and failures to learn. So I take Pat's bar over to Lyle's forge to draw it out, where his master's eye can guide me.

It goes all right at first, then Lyle gets disgusted with my timid hammering. I hold the bar for him and turn it on the anvil as he instructs, and he finishes drawing it out and gives it shape, though he can barely breathe. Then he takes it outside and rubs the hot steel in the dirt, scraping off the scales of carbon to see the colors better as the steel cools. He waits for the right purple-to-tan display and thrusts it into a bucket of crankcase oil.

Lyle's shop is half of his first log building, a dimly lit square with a dirt floor. The other half is the room where Clara shot herself. Lyle thought so little of his first attempt at saddle notches he never bothered to trim the log ends off. In the middle of the floor are the forge and wood heater, whose chimney pipes join, and the anvil. Considerable bench space is taken by homemade machines. One wall is all batteries and two pair of ice skates hanging from the ceiling joist. One wall is a window and a double door. All the projects that failed hang from the remaining two walls, along with some snowshoes and some tools that were made for some job now finished. There is an airplane propeller and a loom. He keeps his failures out where anyone can see them and keeps his successes in drawers. The failures could come in handy someday for parts.

There is really only room for one person to work in here. You have to stand sideways to make it between the workbench and the anvil. The workbenches must have been level when Lyle built them, but now they slope down as if from the enormous weight of minuscule files, pliers, punches, bits, gauges, coffee cans filled with innumerable examples of innumerable categories of small parts, from ordinary nuts, bolts, and screws to lamp generators and carburetor parts for vehicles both extant and extinct.

One window lets in a stingy amount of colorless light. It hasn't been cleaned yet, in forty-five years. It looks like frosted glass with flyspecks. It's a wonder Lyle isn't blind.

He started gun-making with muzzle loaders. He went out on snowshoes in early winter and found a lodgepole pine that had been broken by snow and then had grown back so that the resulting curve was perfect for a pistol grip. He cut that and took it home and spent the next month and a half searching the forest for the Platonic match, the same kind of tree broken to twin the first. The idealization of injury. He knew the lodgepole stands where snow drifts heaviest, breaking the young trees. It looks like a grove of snakes, but he had to cruise a lot of timber to find his mirror grip.

All winter Lyle worked on the forge. He had to make a tap with guides to drill out the barrels to .50-caliber. He made two of everything: triggers, locks, hammers, sights. He roughed out each part on the anvil then filed them down, always applying dissimilar designs to identical specifications. The hammers are identical in weight and stroke, but one is shaped and engraved to resemble a striking cobra; the identical grips are diversely carved. Different parts are tempered to different hardnesses. He made the pins and fittings to remove the barrel, and all the screws. He made the damned screws. In the dim winter light he engraved and polished and blued.

He made a powder horn with brass fittings, two ramrods that fit into holes drilled in the stocks, and a bullet mold. He took the guns out in the yard and fired them enough times to satisfy himself that they were accurate and dependable. Then he carried them inside the house and stuck them in a drawer.

Next Lyle made two rifles, which was harder. He had to design and build a tool to drill a hole three feet long through the center of a steel bar. One after one the winters clicked down. He made two violins, which he called fiddles, starting the same way he did with the pistols, on snowshoes in the woods. He was looking for a straight, even-grained spruce that he could quartersaw two-inch slabs out of to make the carved tops. This time, since they were violins, he made them look the same, but on one he made the back and sides with some maple someone had given him, and the other he made from native wood. He made forms to bend the sides on, a brass thumb plane to shave the braces, and a taper pin reamer to set the tuning pegs. When they were done and tuned, he carried them inside and put them in drawers.

Summers he spent irrigating, haying, and carpentering for neighbors and working around his own place. The winters clicked down with strings of days spent working in the dingy shop, whose benches settled and wore down over forty-five years, hollows like the stone steps of old churches, from the gouges and scratches of files and backsaws, though mostly the bench surfaces were obscured under the sprawl of hand tools that he laid down and reached for without looking up.

He scoured the desert for agates and jade. He made a saw to cut slabs out of stones. He filled several boxes with the cut and polished jewelry he made. Some of the agates are like tiny landscapes with trees and a river or distant mountains under dawn. All women's jewelry—pendants, brooches, earrings—never given or worn. Put away in boxes in a drawer.

Pat Sudeck was raised in New Hampshire. He did a stint
in the Navy, and when he got out it was 1923. In 1923,
there was still land to be homesteaded in the Rockies. He
spent one summer looking over parts of Idaho and northern
Colorado. He may have chosen Colorado near the Wyoming line because of the number of clear nights we have,
and on those clear nights, the number of stars you can see.
I say this because Pat arrived with a telescope and several
years' worth of astronomical journals.

He chose the best section available, half-timber, half-
pasture, with five springs, but no bottomland. It borders the
open prairie, which the maddening wind sweeps clean, so
he could sometimes get to town in winter. It has a view of
the Medicine Bow Range, Snowy Range, Laramie Basin, and
Laramie Peak.

Pat arrived with a horse and wagon. In the wagon were
a woodstove, an army tent, a crosscut saw, a double-bitted
axe, a hammer, a plane, a shovel, the telescope and journals, some food and cooking utensils, and his clothes. He
built a pole floor for his tent, set up the stove, dug out the
spring, and started hand-sawing a winter's supply of wood
and felling the building logs he needed. That first winter he
spent burning wood in the tent, sawing more wood, and
reading astronomy journals by the fire. Not only did he train
his telescope on stars, he turned it on the county road by
the mailboxes seven miles away, to see if anyone had been
out through the snow from town.

He mail-ordered a Belsaw log carriage and a thirty-six-
inch circular ripping blade. He spent the spring putting together his sawmill and ripping the planks for his floor and
roof. Pat bought the motor from an old Packard and used

it to power the sawmill. He used his horse to skid logs out of the woods. By fall his one-room log cabin was done and he went back to bucking up winter fuel.

The second summer he built four miles of perimeter fence so he could rent the pasture for grazing beef. He couldn't go into the cattle business himself without more land and a hay crop, so he devised other strategies instead.

The third summer he dug a root cellar in the sidehill by the spring. Like App Worster and his boys during the same years, Pat had a small vegetable garden, he canned and pickled, and he lived mostly on venison. To get cash for staples and supplies he hired out as a carpenter on ranches that were too far from town to get a union man. He raised goats and mink, especially mink. He bought old horses at the sale barn (live horses are easier to move than dead ones) and slaughtered them to feed his mink. He never quite prospered but he made it to comfortable.

You can tell a lot about someone by how they make things, but you can't tell everything by it. I did some growing up in the house Pat made, and out in the toolshed. I walked past his sawmill every day. I considered his dugout cellars, his springhouse whose water is cold and clear enough to break your teeth, the small alps of whiskey bottles over the back fence.

On the sawmill a system of cables and levers and a horseshoe is bolted to the end of a long rocker arm so that it flops over and cuts the throttle on the Packard. At the other end of the rocker arm a bearing operates centrifugally on the driveshaft as a governor. Pat could operate the motor from the same position he needed to be in to run the logs through the saw and notch them over on the carriage for each board. All the lumber he used he milled on his Packard-powered Belsaw, even shingles.

Pat lived where I live now. He made this house. He preferred the company of stars. I try to imagine his solitude. I try to imagine his loneliness, his endurance. I finger the leather binding on an old pair of snowshoes.

Pat was a good carpenter, but he wasn't much on foundations. He wanted to get to the wood-butchering part so he'd rock up the bottom logs on the corners without masonry, and away he'd go, raising walls and roof, windows, doors, ceiling, floors. He was wild for fancy trim. In his third and last house on this place he made a curved kitchen counter, boards mitered on edge then hand-planed to round, a curved header in the kitchen door, and one bedroom all paneled in aspen. But he never did go back and finish the foundation.

He made beautiful chairs and tables and beds and dressers and mirrors. He chose to spend his one life apart, isolated, self-sufficient. Thirty winters alone; thirty years in the stars.

Pat was a little over five feet tall. He slouched. His face was scrunched up in a clownlike grimace, happy and sad at the same time. Pat drank pure water, wore baggy clothes, and became Lyle's neighbor. He was forgetful. I've found trees half-sawn through standing in the forest, sawlogs cut to length forgotten on the forest floor. Once I found a singletree leaning against a big ponderosa, as if Pat would surely come back for it that afternoon.

When Pat was sixty his doctor told him he had to move to a lower elevation for his health. Pat could see the end of fighting winters alone anyway, so he sold the place to my father for $12,000 and started a cabinet shop in Longmont, a quiet farming town south of Fort Collins. He lived there fifteen years. At age seventy-six, he married for the first time, a woman who owned a motel in Arizona. He spent his last years with his bride, doing handywork around the motel. I remember when news filtered up to Laramie that he'd died.

I only met Pat once. I must have been twelve the one time he came back, before he went to Arizona. He didn't fit the hermit image. He was neither reticent nor gruff. He wore khaki pants and a khaki workshirt. He wore a gray felt hat with a narrow brim. He was soft-spoken and painstakingly polite.

He didn't stay long, a couple of hours. He refused to come inside the house. He talked to my father in the yard. Before he left he took me down to the spring and cut a green willow fork and trimmed it with his pocket knife. We took it up on the mesa and he showed me how to witch water. We walked in circles, me following, through the dry sagebrush. Pat held the live and eager wand. He said, "Nothin' mystical about it. It's just like drivin' a car."

In defense of whatever happens next, the navy of flat-bottomed popcorn clouds steams over like they are floating down a river we're under. To the west, red cliffs, more pasture, the blue Medicine Bow with stretch-marked snowfields, quartzite faces like sunny bone. I'm worried about Lyle getting back from town with his oxygen, but then through binoculars I see him turn the Studebaker, antlike, off the county road and up the four-mile grade, so small down there that I want to imagine his hands on the wheel, still strong, his creased blue jeans and high-top shoes I know he wears to town. He turns off the road on a small knoll about halfway up and stops the truck, facing the mountains. He still looks small against so much space, but I can see his left arm and shoulder and the brim of his hat lowered as he lights a smoke and looks off toward the west, and small countries of light and dark rush across the prairie toward him and over him.

"Ferris became the most popular topic of conversation around coffee tables in ranch kitchens throughout southern Albany County. It wasn't just the aggressively sorry poverty he lived in—a dilapidated mobile home cobbled onto a scrapwood shack with a neoprene roof nailed down with sawmill slabs, leaving the black edges flapping like trapped crows even before the real winds came over the Divide. The real topic of speculation was where did he get all them horses and how did he expect to keep them on forty acres of ridgetop with no water?

"If he spent all day hauling water from the nearest creek he had a right to [Sand Creek was about two miles away], he could keep them and maybe even the goats from dying of thirst, but by early fall he was still hauling in animals and he hadn't begun to bring in any feed. By the end, as I say, he had about twenty of these motley horses, including two stud horses, besides the goats and chickens and dogs and cats and peacocks.

"Forty acres of that kind of high plains pasture could conceivably support two animals if you gave them hay during the winter. Twenty horses would last about two weeks before they'd graze it down to dirt so that it would take twenty years to recover, since we get about fourteen inches of precipitation a year, which is exactly what happened. In two weeks Ferris had himself forty acres of dirt, a personal dust bowl which begun to blow away until he had forty acres of gravel. So you can see why people was wondering what he might have in mind.

"It wasn't long before they found out. What he had in mind was opening the gate. He turned the whole herd out across the Wyoming line, into the old Chimney Rock Ranch.

The first I heard about it was when his studs got into Frank's bunch and cut the hell out of two or three mares, and probably knocked them up with God knows what kind of rough approximation of horseflesh, which Frank didn't much care for, since he is at least as concerned about the looks of his herd as anybody else around here is. You don't want a bunch of blooded quarter horse cow ponies to have some weed of a goosenecked, no-tail, wall-eyed, rhinoceros-looking thing right out in the middle of it. So Clay come out and sewed up the mares where they were cut on the withers, and Frank rode horseback up to have a word with Ferris where he lived on his dazzling junkheap with his hard-looking woman. Frank told me about it later over coffee.

"As Frank's good buckskin gelding carefully picked his way among the refrigerators and shower stalls and even some television sets, the first thing he notices is the smell of goats that even the wind up there couldn't scrub out of the air. The next thing he notices is all the goat sheds Ferris had built, an impressive amount of work even though it was slapdash, like the addition on the trailer where Ferris lived himself, but without the neoprene roofing. It really was a lot of labor, especially when you consider all the junk hauling, poaching, and timber thieving Ferris done on the side. Frank got down, though the goatsmell was fit to suffocate him.

"He knocks on the trailer and Ferris comes out and closes the door behind him, but not before Frank can see that there is an awful lot of stuff—clothes, pots and pans, tools, and cardboard boxes of groceries on the floor, and no furniture. Frank forces himself to shake hands and introduce himself. Then he tells Ferris to round up his horses and keep them fenced and get some hay up there to feed them.

"Ferris was all smiles and squints and apologies. He said he sure didn't know how they'd got out and he'd see to it right away. Then Frank says, 'Listen, Mister, do you know what kind of a place you are living in here? You couldn't have found a windier place on the face of the earth that I know of. What the hell are you thinking about?'

"Ferris just grins, and Frank says, 'Well, you'd better tie all this stuff down before winter or it's going to be spread all over the country by spring, including that sardine tin you're living in.'

"Ferris just squinted and smiled and allowed as how he wasn't afraid of no wind.

"Well, Frank rode home marveling, and ever after that he referred to Ferris as the Goat Man, which kind of stuck with the rest of us, though some referred to him as the Cracker, since he was the first honest to God cracker anybody in these parts had ever seen or mostly even heard of.

"So Ferris collected his stock and shooed them back inside the forty-acre gravel patch where he starved them for a couple of days, and then he turned them out again, this time into Colorado, where he figured the stud horses might stay out of trouble better. But they didn't. They got in with another parcel owner's horses and cut hell out of them, too, though this other outfit was already friends with Ferris and more like him than not, and didn't mind what kind of foals their mares spewed out. They just got him to shoo the herd back onto the gravel patch for another couple of day's starvation before they somehow got out again.

"This went on until the first heavy snowfall, and folks sat around kitchens shaking their heads about what kind of humans had moved in on us and how it sure hadn't taken very long for the country to go to hell."

What we never knew until too late was Ferris never owned them horses. He had duped a lot of people in Fort Collins into *paying* him to 'pasture' them for the winter. If those folks had found out sooner what Ferris meant by pasture, and what was going to happen to their pets when the heavy snows came, they probably would have lynched him on the spot—the only problem being to find a big enough tree anywhere near the Goat Man's digs.

"By January no one knew where the horses were, and if you looked at Ferris's shacks and goat sheds, they were all drifted under about six feet of snow.

"I snowmobiled down that way one morning out of curiosity, and it sure looked abandoned and buried to me, but when I drew up close a dog started barking. I figured Ferris, if no one else, was still there, and I sure as hell had no reason to get any closer than I was. After all, I wouldn't have wanted him sneaking up on me. The wind was humming a lonesome note as I turned around and headed home. It wasn't till spring when I saw Frank again that I heard the end of the story.

"By the time I went down that day and heard the dog bark, Ferris had already left. In fact, when it had snowed a good two feet all in one shot the week before, and then the wind never come to open things up, he and his son had panicked and tried to get out. It took them five days of digging, day and night, to work their pickup down to the plowed county road, and make their getaway back to Fort Collins. The woman wasn't with them (she probably would have made them tough it out). The horses had long been turned out to forage, and several of them had foundered and starved. The goats were all locked up in their pens, froze or

135

starved or suffocated under drifts. The birds all froze. Two dogs and a cat, including that last survivor I heard bark, were locked inside the trailer, where they perished.

"None of this was discovered until a coyote hunter on snowmobile happened to see what was left of the horse herd and called the sheriff, who called Frank, who, together with Ray, hauled several bales of hay up to them using Ray's Trackster and saved them. The SPCA was contacted, and those horses were fed by helicopter till spring, and a warrant was issued for Ferris's arrest.

"Mid-April Frank rode up to the junkpile and found the most grizzly scene he said he'd ever laid eyes on, what with twenty or more animals of various kinds whose frozen carcasses the coyotes had torn apart, except, of course, for the dogs and cat inside the trailer, which had torn each other and the trailer apart in their frenzy.

"When the heavy snow loosened its grip at the end of that month, Ferris just moved back in with a truckload of ammunition and vowed the sheriff would never take him alive. By that time there was a whole county full of ranchers who would have gladly obliged him by taking him in dead just to be helpful. As it turned out though, as things like that usually turn out, he gave himself up without a shot fired.

"By then the roof of his shack had blown clean away and his room was full of snow. He had collected as many goat-parts, chickens, and house pets as he could, and incinerated them right there in the yard, either to get rid of evidence or to get rid of what the evidence would smell like when it thawed. The horses had been rounded up, and the survivors returned to their owners.

"Ferris was sentenced to ten days in the Larimer County Jail and fined a modest fee for cruelty to animals—less than a thousand dollars. Once they had him in the hoosegow they found out he'd been brought up on rape charges two or three times in Collins and had gotten off each time. The wife kicked him out, or off, or whatever—the forty acres had been bought in her name, for reasons one might guess—and Ferris went off in search of more wilderness.

"When the Sand Creek Proprietor's Association demanded that the wife clean up the junk and corpses, she refused, and claimed—and it was borne out—that the shacks and pens and junkpiles were not on her property, but actually occupied an adjacent forty belonging to someone else. The other owner refused to have anything to do with it, since he had never even *seen* his parcel. He was just investing in land with a view.

"So there it sits to this day, glittering like a snowdrift in July, slowly dissipating in gusts of wind, reminding us of what we used to have, how fragile it had been, how little was left of it, and just what kind of a thing it is when people come into the country.

"The last time I seen Ferris I was hauling my oxygen tanks to refill in town. It was mid-May. I still had to shovel a couple of times and use chains to get off the mountain. On the way down the ridge I seen him and his son. They was mired in the spring mud we call gumbo. I suppose they was trying to retrieve something from the trailer; I don't know. I slowed down for a closer look and considered pulling them out, but as soon as they recognized me they started walking guiltily away from their truck, as if they wasn't really stuck at all or in need of a hand, as if they was out to pick wildflowers or hunt arrowheads or something. They slunk a good distance off, so I got back in gear and headed for town.

"By afternoon when I come home the road was a slop-trough of grease. If I'd slipped off the road into the un-packed gumbo, it would have sucked the truck under till it was floating on its running boards. I had to keep momentum to make the hill, or I would have had to back all the way down, a couple of miles, and try again.

"About halfway up the grade I see them again, Ferris and

his son, though neither was what you'd call recognizable. They was covered head to foot in thick red mud. Their truck was about fifty feet from where it had been that morning, off the road, like a sinking skiff.

"They was driving a steel fencepost into the mud, chaining up to it, and hand-winching with a come-along, then jacking out the post again and gaining about three feet with each repetition of the operation. They only had about a mile and a half to go to attain the junkheap. They looked downright aboriginal in their mud suits.

"It wasn't so much that I knew if I slowed down I'd never get up the hill, or that if I left the road to try to pull them out I'd be as stuck as they was. It was just that there are limits.

"This time I just left them there."

138

II.

.II

Frank said, "I guess we do ride a lot. Some ranchers have tried to get away from horses with ATVs and helicopters and such. But it turns out you can't raise cattle without using horses. Not in this country anyway. Horses are cheap, low maintenance, reliable, and they'll go places no vehicle can. Just the kind of places cows like to go.

"So we ride all summer, checking the herd. We move the cows from one pasture to another on horseback, of course. Gathering in the fall entails a lot of riding. We ride when we brand in the spring, and when we sort and pregnancy-test in the fall.

"Sometimes right after haying we get a little free time. That's about the only time of the year where there's a space with not much to do before gathering, winter feeding, and calving. Then we like to take a little time off and go horse-back riding."

Full, the reservoir looks all right: a mirror Sheep Creek dies in, timber straight and still along the edge, and sky swimming through its face.

Drained of water, the reservoir that used to be a hayfield is a barren gravel pit with the dead creek laid out in the bottom of it.

Just below the outlet Sheep Creek resurrects itself in an instant. It leaps from the outlet into boulders, tangled willows, and tall grasses. Below the gunsight rock outcrops that pinch the valley into a waist, Lyle's haymeadow opens like a proper afterlife.

In spring the new grass grows in standing water. At sunset the white mirror-light shines through the grass. That's when the beaver ponds light up, too, and the rising trout make bull's eyes on the surface.

A doe that has been drinking lifts her head to listen. Done irrigating, Lyle heads home across the shining field. He has a shovel on his shoulder that looks like a single wing.

The water we count on is the runoff from high snows gone underground. Some years the rain we get wouldn't fill a thimble. All our streams and springs come from melted snow. After a mild winter the streams are weak by August, so you need a bad winter to have a good year.

A contour map of America shows a heart-shaped basin covering several western states, from southeast Oregon and Idaho down through Nevada and Utah, the real heart of America, where cold air sinks in and fills, like a reservoir of air, until it rises to the spillway and pours through Divide Basin and South Pass like water through a pitcher spout. Only it isn't water, it's all the wind in Wyoming. Snow that settles on open country soon rises into the wind and falls again into the deep timber of mountain ridges where it will be safe. The prairie is often scoured when there's ten feet of snow in the woods.

Ditches they built in the twenties and thirties with dynamite, slips, and mules gather several streams up on Deadman and divert them into the reservoir. Someone has to go up there in the spring and shovel snow out of the ditches to get them running and keep them from washing out. Water is saved behind the dam till they run it out to irrigate the Colorado Plateau. The snow that was saved in the timber is saved again in the reservoir. They sell the water.

In Lyle's meadow a system of ditches girdles the hillside, delineating hay from sagebrush hills. Ditches fork like nerves to reach every part of the meadow. A wooden flume vaults the creek, water crossing water, to irrigate hay on the far bank. Lyle made hay over forty years. It snowed and flooded the meadow. He cut the water off and cut the hay. He saved the hay in the barn. It started to snow again.

Bill McMurray had done virtually nothing but snowshoe back and forth to Deadman between 1948 and 1972. The new water engineer had it all planned out to work hard at the start and get ahead of everything that needed paint or repair. Ray figured when he got a little older things would take care of themselves. He could stay drunk all the time and just read the clocks and turn the wheels on the ditches and dam, which is more or less what happened, only it all happened sooner than expected. There was a period between the hardworking part and the giving-up part where Ray actually tried to moderate his drinking.

One August morning Ray woke about five o'clock with the shakes. Margie was a sleeping mountain next to him in the bed. Nothing could have waked her, but he didn't want to start the day with his usual snort, so he dressed and went out without making a fire or coffee. The air was cold and the sun had not risen above the side of the valley below the dam. The grass was frosted and Ray could see the absolute white where his breath left him for the air.

He went down to the shop and gassed and oiled the chainsaw without making too much of a mess. He loaded the saw and then himself into the pickup, and his little stock dog, Linda, jumped in over his knees. He started the engine without revving it and let the truck roll gently down the hill away from the house. He could barely see through the dog's noseprints on the windshield.

He stopped the truck in the deep meadow grass by the stream below the dam and got out. The grass was white, more like fine bone, and knee-deep. It was like standing in ossified clouds. Ray lit a smoke and watched Sheep Creek, what was left of it, tumble over rocks and stumble into pools, all the water he had gathered from Deadman in his ditches, all the snowmelt he'd laid claim to and saved, then had to turn loose and start over again, shoveling snow out of his ditches in spring.

Ray made an expansive gesture outward with the hand that held the cigarette, and said to no one, "Here we go . . ." Then he made the gesture again and repeated, "Here we go." He walked back through the deep, white, breakable grass to the truck and climbed in. Linda jumped in and resumed her post, forepaws on the dash, nose pressed to the glass.

He drove down the draw to a stand of lodgepoles that had died just his side of Lyle's fenceline. Ray figured if he hauled a load of firewood in and split it for the kitchen stove, that would be worth a drink, maybe even in Margie's eyes. He fired up the Homelite and quickly felled six good-sized trees, all close together so he could back right up to them for loading. He cut the motor on the saw and listened for a minute, then set it down on a stump.

He unsheathed his double-bitted axe, and within half an hour of regular chunking, he had the limbs off all the trees he'd cut. He put the axe away and bucked the tree trunks into sixteen-inch lengths, stopping to sharpen the chainsaw once with a round file, being careful to give each tooth the same number of strokes to keep the chain cutting straight. Then he threw the blocks into the truck bed. They made a level load, which Ray didn't like. He liked a full load, but the hell with it; it was ten-thirty and he was getting pretty thirsty.

He drove the load home and started splitting and stacking the pieces neatly. Every time he swung the axe up over his head, the dry wood fell obligingly in two. He was more than half done when he saw something shiny embedded in one of the split halves. He took out his pocket knife and dug an old bullet out of the wood. The bullet must have struck the tree when it was young since there was no scar in the bark. It had healed over like new. Ray studied the slug. It was an old .44-.40, most likely, no, certainly, from his father's Model '73 Winchester that was up in the bedroom closet. The rifle that jammed that time the bear came after him.

Then Ray thought it couldn't have been. App didn't go around shooting trees, and he would never have missed what he was shooting at. Then Ray figured it out.

The bullet had blown completely through the animal, probably a deer or elk, and had sunk into the tree, which must have been a sapling, since the bullet was near the tree's center. Ray counted rings. They added up. The chances of anyone else discharging a Model '73 Winchester that long ago and right there weren't worth considering.

So the bullet had blown through the body and lodged in the sapling; the sapling healed and grew into a tree and died. Ray felled it, limbed it, blocked it up, and split it, and he had found his father's bullet in the tree's heart. He slipped the mushroom-shaped chunk of lead into his shirt pocket and headed up to the house.

Once they put Hazel in the hospital because she couldn't catch her breath it was a matter of little time. Dad and I would drive Lyle down every day, and Lyle would sit beside her bed and comb her hair with a comb he'd brought. Dad cussed out the nurses for not opening the windows when Hazel asked for fresh air. Hazel mumbled half-coherent words about never giving up, about how love is everything. Lyle combed her hair every day. Death took her asleep.

V*irga* is when rain falls and fails to reach the earth, beautiful and useless as the vista it elaborates. Most angels aren't allowed to touch the ground. We pray for real rain to save the pasture; when it doesn't come we pray for rain to keep the timber from burning. Dry lightning pokes at the timber's green dress. Almost every summer there's a major forest fire somewhere near. Every year we don't disappear in fire we pray our thanks. The summer Lyle died, fires in Yellowstone four hundred miles away smoked us in so we couldn't see the barn from the house. The sun was gone for weeks. It never did rain, though all summer long flotillas of sheepish clouds sailed in and tried to look like rain. They turned dark and sexual. They let down their hair, like brushstrokes on the air, like feathers of water, like the principle it was named for, sublime indifference its gesture, its lovely signature over us.

When I built my own log house in 1980, Lyle wouldn't help me, though he was still healthy then. He wasn't sure I had it in me, and he didn't want the responsibility. What he did was answer all my questions. He explained each step, how to do it and what to watch out for, as I went.

He said there were a couple of trees over on his place that would make good top logs, and I could have them if I wanted. It wasn't really an offer, it was an order. I said I already had logs cut for that. He shook his head and said, "Not big enough. You have to put the biggest log on top."

"Why? Do you need that much more log to hew down flat and notch to take the rafters?"

"No, you have to do it that way because that's how the old-timers done it. The biggest log goes on last."

Once I had the top logs on and had them hewed (trying to work the broadaxe from the elbow like the driveshaft on an old steam train, the way I'd seen Lyle do it), Lyle came over to help me figure the pattern for the rafters. I ripped them out with the handsaw.

It took the two of us, one on each side, to get the first two pairs of rafters nailed to the ridgepole. I was thinking about that. I said, "Lyle, all the buildings you've made by yourself, without any help from anyone, I mean . . . how did you get the first two pairs of rafters nailed without someone to hold them up for you?"

Lyle thought a moment and said, "You know, Jim, I've often wondered that myself."

LYLE, 1974

1/1 Worked in shop—changed batteries in Dodge—fed horses. Several cars on road today. Nice day—18 am soon up to +28.

1/2 Worked in shop—finished draw pull for Don Ruth. Started a pulley for grindstone. Light wind and snow all day—snowed 2 or 3 inches.

1/3 Cleaned chicken house am. Played with motor bike pm. Strong winds—sunny am, cloudy and snow flurries pm. 2 cars on road today.

1/4 Baked bread am—over to Galvin's for lunch—windy but warmer—several cars on road today—think some of them are poachers.

1/5 Went to reservoir am—started to go to Sand Creek but road blowed in. Water line froze up so Ray and I built a bonfire on it—no luck. Windy +18 high.

1/6 Worked on grindstone. Windy day _____

1/7 _____

1/8 Washed clothes am. Worked in shop pm. High wind am. Some snow pm.

1/9 Took pickup over the hill—changed the tank on the freezer—snowing and some wind—about 6" snow. Cold.

1/10 Worked in shop trueing up grindstone. Cold and windy.

1/11 Started working on Ben's desk. Cold today—up to 4 at noon, −18 at 8 pm, light north wind all day.

1/12 Worked on desk—one car on road today— − 10 this am. Warmed up to + 20 this pm—fair wind.

1/13 Baked bread am—Frank Lilley visited pm. Windy but warm—up to + 30 pm.

1/14 Went to Laramie—Oscar gave me 2 pr. Elk hide gloves for Christmas—1 pr. lined—one unlined—sure nice. Windy but warm—above 30.

1/15 Worked on desk. A coon trying to get in chicken house. Set a trap for him. Nice day.

1/16 Worked on desk—coon hasn't been back—Ray came in afternoon. Windy.

1/17 Worked on desk all day. Windy.

1/18 Roy Brown came up and bought the last of the hay, $45.00 a ton. Several cars on road today—2″ snow last night—windy but warm, + 28.

1/19 Worked on desk—saw a coyote chasing a rabbit across the hill—going for all he was worth. Windy all day but warm, + 30.

1/20 Snowed 6″ last night. Worked on desk all day—no wind but getting cold tonight—down to − 22 at 9 o'clock.

1/21 Ray was here today—brought the mail and some milk—a real nice day, + 14 at six am, up to + 32 pm. Getting windy tonight. Worked on desk.

1/22 Same old thing—windy and warm.

1/23 Same old thing—windy as hell and snow flurries. + 28.

1/24 Same old thing—windy as hell— + 32—a pickup on road today.

1/25 *Same old thing.*

1/26 *Lots of tourists running around today—Warm and windy +38.*

1/27 *Worked on desk—snowed 4" last night—east wind and cold today, +4 tonight.*

1/28 *Patched overalls and done some cooking—snow flurries and light wind, +28—wind rising tonight.*

1/29 *Broke the shuttle carrier on the sewing machine—hope I can make another one—clear day up to +28 some wind.*

1/30 *Went to town—Ray and Margie were here for supper—sure nice to have someone to eat with—East wind tonight and +4, snowing some. Started repairs for sewing machine.*

1/31 *Went to reservoir for dinner—almost had to shovel to get back. Windy and snow moving—up to +25—guess I'll have to start using the snowmobile.*

2/1 *Worked on desk—have it nearly cleaned off—a tourist on road today. Clear and windy, up to +20.*

2/2 *Ray, Jack, and Ki were here pm. Baked bread and worked around house am—in shop pm making part for sewing machine— – 8 this morn, +32 at noon.*

2/3 *Cleaned chicken house, Frank came and stayed all day—windy am, quiet pm.—warm.*

2/4 *Finished part for sewing machine and it works—pulled a guy out of the snow, he tried to give me $10.00—no wind but cloudy and cool, up to +20.*

2/5 *Worked on desk—done some sewing and loafed—cold and windy—some snow flurries.*

2/6   This day wasted. Windy and cold.

2/7   Worked on desk—the wind blew like hell all day—up to +22. The white cactus in blossom tonight.

2/8   Worked on desk—windy and some snow flurries, +30.

2/9   Sig Palms and three other game wardens visited today. Worked on desk putting it together. Windy and warm, +37.

2/10   Baked bread and worked on desk—windy and snow flurries, 28.

2/11   Three cars on road today, damn tourists wasting gasoline, guess they think there's no end to it, damned fools. Windy and warm.

2/12   Worked on desk in am—walked over to pickup in pm—put on new license plates, warm and windy, up to 38—windy as hell tonight.

2/13   Worked on desk am—Ray and Ki were here pm—I sawed some wood. Warm nice day.

2/14   Worked on desk, windy—colder and snowing.

2/15   Worked on desk am—got out the Ski-doo and checked it over and went over the hill. Had about 4" snow.

2/16   Baked some pineapple kolacky am—worked on desk pm. Nice day and warmer +22.

2/17   Worked on desk—2 cars on road today—they can only get this far. Cold, some wind.

2/18   Went to town, saw some elk over the hill. Ray and Jack were here for supper. Cold and windy, +4 this morn.

2/19   Sanded the desk and put on another coat of varnish—Windy; not very warm.

2/20   Patched overalls.

2/21   Baked bread and washed some clothes am—remodelled a shirt pm. Cold day +10

2/22   Just tinkered around—windy and cold. −16 am, +10 pm.

2/23   53 years today, patched underwear am, overalls pm—snowed some this morn and was cold, but cleared and warmed up to +3 this pm.

2/24   Put the third coat of varnish on desk—windy but clear and warm +38.

2/25   Don Ruth came today, Stayed all day, I didn't get a damned thing done. Warm and clear.

2/26   Didn't do anything today either, Jesus I feel tired and lonely. Warm day but windy, +32.

2/27   Charged batteries in Dodge and fed the horses—put the last coat of varnish on desk, looks good. Windy and colder, snow flurries.

2/28   Damn tourist came up the creek and got stuck in the snow. Took him an hour of shoveling to get out. They don't have any sense at all. Warm and windy.

2/29   This day ain't on my calender.

3/1   Started sewing up a pair of P.J.'s am—sawed wood in pm. Two cars on road today—real warm, +42, some wind.

3/2   Spent the whole day reading, sure lazy.

3/3   Ray, Jack, and Ki were here this morning, came back this evening, stayed till late. Nice day. Bluebirds arrived today.

3/4 Fixed horse trophy for Frank's mother am, looked for old pictures pm. Snow in am 1½" —Clara's birthday.

5/27 Went to the Johnson place to start building the scale house. Fairly nice day but cool.

5/28 Stormy—East wind and light snow. Stayed home and done some cooking.

5/29 Snowed last night. Have nearly 16" since yesterday am. Went up to check the ditch and over to see Galvins. Whiteout. Hard to see.

5/30 Stayed home and rested and filed a saw. Took the Ski-doo to check the fence, scared some elk out of the draw. Nice day and warm.

5/31 Worked in shop and spent some time with the water. Nice day, some fog early.

6/1 Irrigated all morning. Went to Frank's and mail box pm—nice day.

6/2 Went to town.

6/3 Worked at the Johnson on the scales.

6/4 Worked on scales

6/5 Worked on scales

6/6 Worked on scales

6/7 Worked on scales

6/8 The next 5 days I worked on the scales.

6/9 _____

6/10 _____

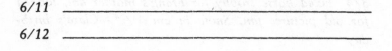

6/11 _____

6/12 _____

6/13 _____

6/14 Claude brought his cows up today.

12/6 Snowing today—worked on grindstone shaft bearings.

12/7 Still snowing—have about 6". Jimmy Galvin and Julie came over in afternoon.

12/8 J. Galvin Sr. came today with his woman. Forgot her name.

12/9 Cleaned chicken house—shut off Marie's spring—put new wire glass on south bay window—washed outside windows—charged light batteries.

12/10 Went to town then res for supper. Nice day but cold— – 14 in morning.

12/11 Baked bread, trimmed the geraniums, put coasters on sewing machine. Ben and Don came in morning. Ray and Margie at noon. Van Freemont and wife in afternoon. Windy day.

12/12 Went to Galvin's, saw five coyotes—over to Marie's cabin to cut tree—took tractor to barn in afternoon. Windy.

12/13 Went down to Johnson place to fix water pipes—went to town with Mrs. White—cloudy most of day—snowed some late afternoon.

12/14 Cold and windy today—cleaned the bay window—recovered the shelves and washed the windows.

12/15 Worked some on grindstone—walked up to feed horses—Worster tribe here in evening—cold and windy, some snow flurries.

12/16 Washed clothes in am worked on grindstone in pm. Cold and windy.

12/17 Got my Christmas cards ready and went to town—went to see Ray on his job, sure a mess—Nice in am, colder, stormy pm.

12/18 Made a double throw switch for batteries. Worked on grindstone trying to get it to run true. Cold and windy.

12/19 Put the control on the windcharger, got it going. Hooked up the new batteries. They are Western Electric—cost $25.00 each. Cold and wind.

12/20 Worked in shop, chipping grindstone to true it up. Cold and windy—snow flurries. Hooked on new batteries today.

12/21 Worked in shop making another switch and chipping on grindstone. Windy as hell but warmer.

12/22 Worked in shop—went up to feed horses am—Ray and Harold were here in pm—late in day 12 Jeeps and a pickup went down. Cold and windy, +10 high.

12/23 Baked bread and other cooking in am. Worked in shop in pm. −10 this noon, some light snow, east wind tonight.

12/24 Worked in shop am. Frank and Clay were here pm. −18 this morning. Windy afternoon. At 8:30 pm, 0 degrees, strong wind.

12/25 Christmas! ha! Not a soul did I see this day.

12/26 Calm and sunny. Worked in shop making a stone-

facing hammer to smooth up the grindstone. Ray and Marge were here for supper. Marge gave me a willow cup for Christmas.

12/27   Worked in shop am. Went to reservoir for dinner. Nice in am, cloudy in pm.

12/28   Went to town—stopped to visit with Don Collins on the way home—Don is 74 years old and looks good. Nice day but cool.

12/29   Baked bread—worked some in shop and rested. Nice day—cold in am, – 8.

12/30   Worked in shop on a pair of spurs for Don Ruth. Sure a SOB to make. Some wind but nice, up to 20.

12/31   Worked in shop am—went for a walk pm. Some light snow am, sunny pm. A lonesome time of year.

Since the first time App went to sleep, in that strangely cold, green place with his old man, on the Sheep Creek side of Boulder Ridge, he had a desire to go back there and build a ranch on that spot. It was a feeling like he belonged there, that the events of his life would inevitably lead him back, and he would be happy. It was as though he had a tuning fork vibrating in his chest when he thought about it.

It didn't, therefore, worry him much when someone else laid claim to 360 acres of the meadow, including some side-hill pasture and a good bit of the bordering timber.

That was 1895. In 1895, App knew, there were many places that, from a practical point of view, would have made better homesteads than that one, places down out of the heavy snow country and a lot closer to town. App liked that Sheep Creek meadow from an impractical point of view. It was like a separate country. It was a place where he could disappear into the mountains, into a life that was no one else's, where he didn't need anyone to get by. Furthermore, App didn't consider thirty miles from town any more than far enough from town. When he was twenty he rode the fifty miles from Laramie to Virginia Dale and back on a horse named Spook in less than six hours on a bet.

When he heard that some stranger had filed on the piece of ground his heart was set on, that almost imaginary thatch of peat bog surrounded by low hills and tall stands of lodge-pole pine, with its own ocean of sage-gray prairie lapping at its shores and the whole Medicine Bow Range to drink in every day, he just started to figure how he could get it *back*.

Except in the rare instance of an App Worster, who preferred the absence of people to the people themselves, whenever you see someone living that far from human society, human scrutiny, chances are they are not so much hiding as hiding out. Chances are they are temporary. The best thing for App to do was to save his money, since he'd have to buy the place now, if not from the homesteaders then from the bank. That was number one. Number two was to find a wife, since a man who likes solitude doesn't necessarily like loneliness, and the help would be a plus.

There was a girl in Laramie who gave App that same tuning fork feeling in his chest whenever he saw her, which was usually when he went into the eating house across from the Union Pacific station, where she worked. Saving for a ranch was antithetical to the indulgence of store-bought dinners, but it was the only way he could talk to her and get that hum inside his chest. Besides, App was a man of unusual intelligence and energy, and could make pretty good money bringing deer and elk meat to the town, trapping some, and occasionally hiring on to break colts on ranches.

When the news came out that whoever was living up there on Sheep Creek was wanted in Oklahoma for robbery, and had been supplying Jack Slade with different horses to ride so that he would be harder to recognize when he knocked over a small town bank, App wasn't surprised. It seemed like destiny. He had to ride to Fort Collins to sign for the deed. He bought the place outright. The price was four hundred dollars. Then he walked into the lunchroom and asked Marie to marry him.

Her eyes were dark green. She was shy and rarely spoke. Her waist was so thin App could encircle it with his hands, so that his thumbs and middle fingers touched.

Though their acquaintance was slight by modern standards—mostly abashed, brief pleasantries—a girl stranded in a frontier town had limited time and opportunity. So when App asked her, and told her about the ranch, she and her mother agreed they should marry.

Nevertheless it was with more fear than excitement constricting her breath and making her heart flutter that she climbed onto the wagon seat next to App after their ten minutes in front of the Justice of the Peace. They creaked and rattled out of town onto the thirty miles of barely visible track and then no track at all across the prairie toward the green hills to start a life together.

All Marie could think about as they rolled across the Laramie Basin and then began to climb toward Boulder Ridge were stories she knew to be true about girls coming all the way from the East or Europe, where they'd had decent, respectable lives, coming west on the promises of men who claimed to be rich landholders, gentlemen with mansions and vast herds of cattle or sheep. Men who met these girls at the station in St. Louis or Denver, married them on the spot, and then, swigging whiskey and spitting nonstop, drove them into the desert and whoaed up in front of some board shack or hole in the ground with a roof, like where a badger might live, with floors and walls of dirt, and without a tree or even a hill in any direction. They'd had to winter in such burrows, wide awake in the shrill whiteness of the outer world where they would die in a matter of hours if they tried to escape and be torn apart by wolves. Many women lost their minds in such circumstances, or took their own lives.

When App pulled up short at the top of the ridge, just as the sun was setting over the deep green meadow with the creek running through it and wildflowers smattering the sidehills and a decent log house with a bay window facing south, her fears melted into most delightful, from App's point of view, manifestations.

It was a good house, well made of logs, with a steeply pitched roof to shrug off heavy snows, three rooms, and a strangely fancified bay window that made the living room almost too hot in the winter sun, even when the outside temperature was well below zero. "Some of them thieves was pretty handy with the axe," App remarked. "I guess nobody's all bad."

The sun shines an average of 340 days a year on Boulder Ridge. That's why it has that dried-up and about-to-blow-away look and all the white light, and why Marie was so taken with the lush green of the Sheep Creek meadow. There are bigger meadows down on the Laramie River, but they're surrounded by empty sage flats. They don't have that protected feeling.

Marie liked the house and the first winter wasn't bad. They were able to visit her mother three times between November and May, when the wind carved a passage through the drifts. But App didn't care for the location of the house or its size—or so he said. What he meant was he hadn't built it himself.

The former owners had begun a big log barn at the upper end of the meadow, but they'd quit before they got the top logs and the roof on. App decided to finish the barn and build a house next to it, and put the sheds and corrals he'd need to raise cattle up there, too, so that everything would be together and handy for winter feeding. He spent his next year getting that done (and planting a family) but the barn is all that's left of what App built at the upper end of the meadow.

The barn is something of a puzzlement. Clearly it was not begun by the same hand that built the house below.

162

Whoever started the barn didn't have a very good idea of how it's supposed to be done. The corners are saddle-notched, but all the cups are turned up instead of over, so they catch the rain water and tend to rot out. Those logs can roll in their cups and the barn spits them out with the passage of time. Well, most of the log buildings in America were first tries, but I've always wondered what happened to the fellow who built that house. He wasn't around when they started the barn; he wouldn't have allowed such methods.

It's easy to see where App's work begins on the barn: The vastly oversized top logs are hewn flat on the outside with a broadaxe so expertly it looks like they were milled, planed, and sanded. The rafters are hewn square and notched snugly into the top logs and pegged down to keep the roof from lifting like an enormous wing into the wind (though once when Lyle owned it the wind got so fierce it *did* lift the roof and three top logs and set it over a foot or so).

App finished the barn, which is thirty-by-sixty-feet, in the second summer. He filled it with stalls, and the loft with hay, and brought up a starter herd of old-fashioned long-horned cows and calves. App's stock spread up Sheep Creek to Bull Mountain and down Sand Creek to Chimney Rock. It was easier to keep an eye on them from a horse than to build enough fence to keep them home.

Ray had an enormous old photograph, maybe twelve-by-twenty-four inches, of the new house App finished in time for his first child to be born. Marie is standing in the doorway with the infant in her arms. The hay barn still looks about the same as it does in the picture, but today there's no trace of the house or any of the sheds or corrals. The house and the rest of it burned down one year after it was finished. A chimney fire set the shake roof ablaze while App was cutting hay among the willows with a scythe, cleaning up the tight spots where he couldn't mow with the team.

He looked up once and everything was tranquil, smoke from the cookstove lazing into the sky. The next time he looked up the roof was engulfed in flames and Marie was running in her long dress across the yard with Goldie in her arms, the child's swaddling trailing smoke.

They moved back down to the house with the bay window, but a series of hard winters kicked something out of Marie's spirit and she became consumptive. The winter Goldie was three and Marie was pregnant with Pete, they weren't able to get to town for five months. Game was scarce and they survived mostly on venison jerky. Marie just wasn't built for winters like that, so far away, nor summers stacking hay, canning, sewing, gardening, and cooking. After Pete was born she never got out of bed again.

App sold off stock to pay for doctors' calls and medicine. The medicine was mostly laudanum, a mixture of opium and alcohol that was easily available, but whose beneficial effects were questionable. The last summer she was alive, App spent most of his time digging a thousand feet of ditch, six feet deep, from the spring down to the house. He swung the pickaxe and shoveled fourteen hours a day. It kept his mind off what was happening. When the ditch was finished he made a thousand feet of wooden pipe out of lodgepole rails drilled in the middle and threaded on the ends. He wanted it so that if Marie ever recovered she would never have to haul water in a bucket again.

To this day no one has been able to figure how App drilled out those poles into sections of pipe ten and twelve feet long without coming out the sides, but he did it. Lyle found many of those pieces still in place when he dug up the line fifty years later and put down PVC. No one knows why they never rotted either, since they were buried and untreated.

Marie's health slipped steadily, and it depressed App so much that, after the water line was in, he more or less gave up tending to things. Marie's sister came to the ranch to take care of her, and after Marie died and App lost the ranch, App married the sister. She bore two children in the claim shack, and then she died, too, and that was the end of App's dream.

Ray and Jack were born in that claim shack at the base of Boulder Ridge, near Tie Siding. When their mother died App sent all four children to the third and last sister, who lived in eastern Washington. The boys eventually came back, but Goldie never did. For the rest of his life App had to picture Marie carrying her from the burning house with her blankets still smoldering.

Ray said his father never got over losing Marie, the girl whose waist was so slender he could encircle it with his hands, like the low hills of timber surrounding the meadow. Ray said App never stopped thinking about Marie his whole life, never stopped missing her. The day she died App climbed up on a haystack in the middle of the meadow and lay there on his back for three days and nights, facing the sky. Ray said he lay on that haystack and cried.

As far as I know Ray never did anything worse than drink too much, smoke, and curse, and occasionally take an elk out of season—except for once. It was at a dance at Woods Landing where the Worster boys were providing the music (Pete on fiddle, Ray and Jack on guitars and singing—this would have been 1960). There was a bully in there—a usual sort of smalltime bar brawler who started fights in saloons the way other people go bowling on Saturday nights—insulting people and generally trying to get something started. People were only afraid of him because of the pure joy he seemed to derive from beating someone up, always someone smaller or drunker than he was.

That night he made the mistake of picking a fight with Ray, who was both smaller and drunker, and who ordinarily walked away from invitations like that, but the guy insulted Margie instead of Ray, and she was sitting right there and heard it. Not that she gave a damn, but Ray did, and the two men agreed to go outside in the snow. As they reached the door the guy said, "Ray?" and when Ray turned around the guy let him have it, and as soon as Ray had picked himself up off the floor, he did it again. "Ray?" Bang.

Once they got outside in the snow Ray not only slapped tar out of that bully, but once he was ready to give up, begging for mercy, Ray put a hammer lock on his head with one arm and went to work on the guy's face with the other. When I say work I mean a long and steady kind of work like a hammer breaking rock, steady, methodical blows as if Ray actually expected the man's head eventually to crack in two. When Ray let him drop there was not much recognizable about his face.

That was the only time Ray actually hurt anybody, but Ray had a feeling they were saving a place for him in hell, and he made his list of questions for the Devil.

By 1975 Lyle had finished reading much of the Laramie library and was having the Denver library sent up a dozen books at a time. He was not limited by subject matter or genre; he had total recall.

He liked Homer, Tolstoy, Dickens, stories "about people's doin's." He hated Dostoyevski and Faulkner. About the former he remarked, irritated, "All them people is nuts." About Faulkner: "If that sumbitch wants to tell me a story why don't he start it at the beginning and tell it through to the end?" He liked James Wright: "Me and him get along."

One of his main interests was religion and theology, though he subscribed to no doctrine. He'd read the subject through from the fundamental to the occult. He was curious about the kinds of answers given by people who thought they had answers. He himself had none, but he always gave others the benefit of the doubt, from Jesuits to Sikhs, and he was always disappointed.

When zealous fundamentalist missionaries of various stripes found out there was this old man way back up on Sheep Creek whose soul needed saving and who wouldn't slam the door in their faces but would actually invite them in for coffee, there was a big run on Lyle's soul. Ray was dead by then or they surely would have worked him over, too. The Pillar of Fire, Jehovah's Witnesses, Nazarenes, and Mormons—all sent delegations the fifty miles up the mountain from Collins and were greeted warmly and without prejudice by the old "hermit" who lived in the emerald valley and whose eyes were the color of the farthest peaks you could see from the ridge top.

Lyle listened with limitless patience to their Bible quotes and what they thought it all meant. Then he asked them a few lethal questions that sent them scurrying through the pages of their pamphlets hunting for the scripture that might save them. It always ended with the prophets unnerved and Lyle disappointed because he wanted answers and wasn't getting any.

The Watchtower started coming in the mail and the Witnesses sent him a rescue team of three pretty women; the oldest forty and the youngest fourteen. They brought him sweet rolls and they giggled a lot and they sure hoped he'd drive down country one day before it was too late and have his soul saved by Reverend So and So. When they left Lyle said, "What a waste of perfectly all right womanflesh."

Then the Pillar of Fire started in on him, reading their pamphlets and claiming that they had the word of God and no one else did, which pricked Lyle's curiosity. He asked them what they thought of Mormons, and they replied, "Oh, that's just a cult."

Then Lyle said, "Now wait a darn minute. You say you have the word of God from Moses, who was a Jew that went up on that mountain and brought down the Ten Commandments, right?" Nods all around.

"Well, Joseph Smith found the golden tablets and showed them to his people the same way, and they are no more gone than Moses' tablets, and Joseph Smith said that was the word of God, so what's the difference? The word of God came to Mohammed and told him it was all right to prey on the caravans, which he done, so what's the difference?"

He asked a number of questions that were beyond their frame of reference. Finally, more as a last-ditch strategy than out of goodwill, they asked Lyle if he'd ever been baptized. Lyle said he didn't know, which he didn't. They started in on him to go down to Sheep Creek right now to make sure.

Lyle said he wouldn't go because he wasn't convinced of anything. "And besides," he said, "if I *am* already baptized I sure don't want a dunk in that ice water for nothing." He stubbed out his cigarette and said, "You know, that water comes right out of the bottom of the reservoir, and it's not much warmer than the snow it's made from." He smiled wide, showing them the gold linings in his teeth. He said, "That water is so cold, Preachers, it'd make your old balls draw up to where you'd never find 'em again." And he just kept smiling as they swept up their pamphlets, bobbed a hurried thanks for coffee, and fled.

It still rankled Lyle, though, how much time he'd spent with them, and how frustrating they were to talk to, how they seemed to have no real affection for the truth. The next day he told me all about it and said, "You know, if heaven is filled with them dummies, I'd just as soon go down to hell and be with Raymond."

My wife showed Lyle pictures of the house where we'd lived for a while in Italy. Lyle wanted to know about the wall around the Umbrian hilltop town. Was there mortar in it originally? Jorie said she didn't know, but she didn't guess so. Lyle said, "That's strange, because by the eleventh century the Roman mortaring techniques had made their way up as far north as Umbria."

There was no need to check on it.

My friend Billy Embree's family used to own the Mountain Meadow Ranch on the Laramie River. It's just a dude ranch now, but Billy's grandfather had homesteaded it, and when we were kids it was still in his family. The foreman was a man named Arch McLean. Arch only had a thumb and two fingers on his right hand. He made a point of shaking hands with us kids every chance he got.

Summers we horsebacked through the big meadows and up the draws at the base of Jelm Mountain. We fished in the Laramie River; we massacred jackrabbits with our .22s. But we also liked being treated like men. We wanted to learn to be good hands.

So when Arch went out to build fence or check the herd, we went with him. It was before they sprayed the Laramie River, and the damned mosquitos were so thick between mid-June and the first of August, it was hard to hear above their drone. If you didn't wear a bandana over your mouth and nose you were going to breathe a lot of them. Billy and I drenched ourselves in 6-12 repellent, which seemed to have a mild deterrent effect, but Arch never used it. He said, "Billy, what would your grandfather say if he saw you smearing that sissy-ass perfume on you?"

Arch had somehow transcended mosquitos. Out building fence one day, setting cedar posts and stretching wire, we tried to help him but had to retreat to the cab of the pickup every so often to get away from the insects that covered us with welts despite bandanas, bug dope, and denim shirts buttoned all the way up and all the way down.

Arch kept up a steady pace without ever bothering to brush them away. He didn't cover his nose and mouth. They never bit him, either, as far as I could tell, just landed on him. That day, working the spud bar, you couldn't see an inch of flesh beneath his hat. His face was a mask of gray wings.

App sits in the open doorway of the claim shack with his bum leg in the sun, slowly rubbing it up and down and thinking. It is only the first of March, but when the sun shines with no wind it is always hot. App thinks his swollen, stiffened leg is like a tree trunk that the early spring warmth will draw the sap up into.

As he sits in the doorway hour after hour he tries to make himself remember only the good things, tries for a little warmth in his soul. He'd started out pretty strong, as strong and capable as any man. He'd had a beautiful young wife, a green mountain ranch, children, cattle, horses, hay, and he'd lost it, or most of it, just by trying to hang on. He'd married a second time, but the hard luck dogged him and the doctor bills and lean years ended up taking everything he'd dreamed and found and built, except for his three boys.

He tries to concentrate on the early days, before the run of hard winters and disease. In those days he used to wake each morning feeling completely indestructible. The good green memories, those warm winter sunshine memories make him smile in the sunlight with his eyes closed, and he can see the moving pictures of the times they made love down by the flume he'd built to irrigate the patch of meadow on the far side of the creek. Right out in the open sunshine in the greenness of all the different kinds of grasses that still grew in that meadow. They could hold hands and run buck naked through all that green with no way in hell anyone was going to see them cutting up like damn fool kids. But it was living that far away that killed her, App thinks, that sent her farther away yet, like she is now, only reachable in memories and dreams.

The smile has left his face and he opens his eyes and looks

down at the lumber his leg has become, sticking out the front door into the barren sunshine, and he looks down at the legs of his wooden chair sunk slightly into the dirt floor of the claim shack that isn't his, that is built on a strip of land between two borders that two states refused to claim, and he thinks of the cold cellar dark out back, hung with jerked venison, and with a small hill of blind potatoes. He bakes six each morning in the coals of the heater and gives two to each of his boys as they leave in the Model-T for school, to warm their hands until they get there and to eat for lunch.

Suddenly a little breeze picks up and makes App shiver, then a small cloud covers the sun and chills him through. He starts to think of the time on Sheep Creek when he told Marie to wait supper for him, when three feet of snow had fallen during the night and it was just the end of October. He still had cows up near Bull Mountain. Most of them were smart enough to come down when it snowed, but not all. He decided to ride out and bring the stragglers down.

The horse's belly dragged in the snow, but it was a light, dry powder. The horse was strong and plowed through the drifts with his head down like a doubtless pilgrim. App's boots were making their own runnels alongside the horse's big furrow. The weather seemed like it would hold clear and cold, and he didn't notice that his feet were frozen by the time he made it up to the big meadow on Sand Creek where he expected to find his strays. They were nowhere to be seen so he pushed on when he should have turned home. His legs were numb all the way to his knees before he realized they were cold. So intent had he been, scanning the hypnotic white ridges and draws for his stock, that it was near dark before he knew that he'd gone too far, that he was in trouble.

His horse was still strong, but they were too far from any timber to build a fire, the snow was deep, and he could not feel anything from the waist down.

He rode into an arroyo and up the other side. He saw a

174

young antelope, not yet a yearling, separated from the herd somehow, standing above him on a high spot of ground. She was unable to go anywhere, unable to reach the grass beneath the snow anymore, so played out and exposed that she just stood there shivering like a wet dog on the back porch, looking right at App, too tuckered out to run or show any fear.

App rode slowly up to the antelope child. Since he could not dismount any more than the antelope could run, he dropped the loop of his lariat over the antelope's neck and hoisted her up onto the saddle and laid her across his legs like a lamb. Then he turned his horse for home. His legs thawed out some because of the critter on his saddle, and the antelope decided she liked it better where she was now than where she was before. She never struggled when App carried her into the house after midnight and laid her in his wife's lap.

The antelope that App figured had saved his life got named Misty. She hardly went out of the cabin that winter, but lapped up pans of sugared milk and ate hay from Marie's hand. Misty slept on a blanket next to the stove. By spring she was going outside to graze on the new shoots of grass making their way up through the sagebrush, and she knew to come when called by name.

That summer they left her outside nights. She'd bed down and disappear in the sage until Marie said her name. Then she'd spring up, long-legged and skittish, and bounce up to lick the salt from Marie's palm.

When the antelope herded up that fall, App wondered what Misty would do. She went with them. One morning the following summer, though, Marie said an antelope ewe with twins at her side came strangely near the cabin, sniffed, and kind of perked up when Marie called "Misty" and held out her hand. Then she bolted and ran with the two miniatures of herself zigzagging and playing tag like two kites she was trying to get to fly.

The Overland Stage ran up from Fort Collins, through Virginia Dale, to Tie Siding, where it veered west to the Wooden Shoe and on up north for the Pass.

Jack Slade kept the roadhouse at Virginia Dale. As stationmaster he always knew when there was money on board and, of course, when the stage was due to arrive. He'd saddle a new fast horse, of which he kept several, supplied by an outfit on Sheep Creek that wasn't exactly buying them first. He'd trot down to Owl Canyon, where the stage had to snake through a narrow sandstone canyon on a steep upgrade. With a bandana covering his face dime-novel-style, Slade would leap aboard the passing coach from the overhanging rocks. He would come up on the drivers from behind, armed, tell them to whoa and not turn around. He would relieve the coach of its hazard of cash and jump down to disappear into the rocks. He then retrieved his mount and rode hell for leather back to Virginia Dale on a side trail he'd worked out. By the time the stage pulled into the station, shouting the news, Slade had his feet propped up on the porch rail and would take it all in with feigned astonishment. His horse was cooling down in the barn. Slade pulled that trick regularly over a number of years, letting most of the cash get through for appearance's sake and not wanting to overgraze his pasture. He finally retired out of boredom.

Not that Jack Slade was funny. After he left here he went to Julesburg where he tied a man to a corral fence and shot him in the groin and both knees and left him. No one knows why.

The old town of Tie Siding was right on the Union Pacific track, seventeen miles southeast of Laramie, seven miles north of the Colorado line. The Boulder Ridge Road runs southwest from Tie Siding about twenty miles up into Colorado. It was a major logging road that the UP's oxen and tie wagons made when the tracks first came through. They cut the ties up here to put on flatcars at Tie Siding, using the track they'd already built to supply construction into the tieless prairie northward and westward. The railroad kind of built itself like that, sending roadroots into the timber, budding railroad flowers like Tie Siding, sending out new branches, drawing nourishment along its length. Ties from Boulder Ridge and rails from Pennsylvania, our timber sent up to bed new track as far as Rock Springs.

Once the railroad finished growing itself, Tie Siding started to die. When Ray started school, the school was the only building not boarded up. The town had once sported three saloons and two whorehouses. When Ray was in second grade they built a new Tie Siding about a mile away, on the old stage trail, which had become U.S. Highway 287, connecting Laramie and Fort Collins, and they moved the school, too.

Miss Gunnerson became Tie Siding's schoolmistress around 1927 when the town was still by the tracks. Pat Sudeck was homesteading on top of the ridge, and Lyle Van Waning was a five-year-old playing in the dirt on the floor of a sod house. Miss Gunnerson was the only teacher Ray ever had.

She also ran the post office and pumped gas. Until she left, sometime in the sixties, she *was* Tie Siding, living there alone in that cluster of small white buildings, like woodchips washed up from a lake of sagebrush, ringed all around by distant mountains. Ray said she was always too nice to punish anyone. She got the rowdy ranch kids to behave by shaming them into it. I never asked what became of Miss Gunnerson. I just wonder what it must have been like for her to leave after forty years of giving children their lessons in the wind.

One year the Worster boys never went to school because the ridge stayed open all winter. Ordinarily, though, there was plenty of foul weather to go to school in. It was just that they didn't start till December and would be back on the mountain swinging their axes by April. App would put them back to work whenever there was a spell of fine weather. Ray quit the eighth grade when he got too big for the desks.

In October of 1958 Ray donated a new coat of stucco to the schoolhouse. The men who volunteered to help from the nearby ranches were mostly Ray's old schoolmates, now wind-parched cowboys in their thirties. Waiting for a load of sand they stood around smoking and chewing and drinking coffee out of thermos lids. They were joking and arguing about who used to whip whose ass when they were boys in school. Ray allowed as how none of them would tease Jack about being harelipped now. Indeed, Jack had grown bigger and stronger than any of them, but it wasn't that alone that put respect in their voices when they talked about him. They were grown men now. Their lives were not easy. Now they shared something more than the world's largest supply of sagebrush and wind.

Ray said, "I bet Jack could lift a thousand pounds."

The joking turned serious and bets were made. The next thing Jack was picking up sacks of cement. He held two sacks pinched between his legs. They started handing him more and loading him down, two sacks under each arm.

Then he bent over so they could stack cement sacks on his back. They put four sacks on his back. That was it. He held it, a thousand pounds.

Jack let the sacks fall to the ground, then he straightened, smiling, and said, "How was that, Raymond?"

Ray dragged his sleeve across his eyes.

Till the day he died Ray never missed an opportunity to sing for an audience, never mind being blind drunk and unable to make it all the way through any given song without forgetting the words. He had a clear, strong voice, a good range. Ray always sang from the heart, no artifice. Pete fiddled, Jack harmonized. I believe the only reason they never went professional was because no one outside Laramie in the late thirties and early forties had heard of them, and they'd never heard of themselves either. It never occurred to them that they might make the big time with the backward kind of cowboy swing they played, so they played saloons and barn dances on weekends.

For ten years it was a party every Saturday at my father's house, Pat's third cabin, starting when the Worsters moved in over at the reservoir, which was the summer Hazel died.

Two or three months after his mother died, and he'd got his grieving somewhat done (he was exactly fifty then), Lyle went through a period of jubilant freedom most people get done with before they are twenty. But Lyle never had the chance before, so he quietly went happy-haywire for about three years.

The first thing Lyle did after he buried his mother was buy a motorcycle from a kid in town. It was during the fuel shortage, and Lyle said he'd save money by running his fences and ditches and visiting neighbors on the Suzuki 150 instead of always taking the truck, which was true enough, but it never fooled anybody.

Lyle always came for the company on those Saturday nights. He'd take a little watery rum and nurse it all night while Ray put down a quart easy, pulling between songs. Lyle never sang. Sometimes he'd help Ray remember lyrics, and he tapped his foot and seemed to enjoy himself.

I saw a photograph once of Lyle sitting on the running board of an old Dodge pickup, playing a mandolin. His brother, Henry, was standing over him listening, his foot propped on the running board, too, and his hat brim pulled down low over his eyes. I asked Lyle if he played the mandolin, and he said he did but not in public. It was hard for me to imagine anyone with hands the size of Lyle's playing the mandolin, his fingers too massive to press a single pair of strings, and he allowed as how that had been a problem. But he could pick out tunes.

That night Ginny, Lainie, Bill, Jack, Shirley, and Dave were there, too, whooping it up. Lyle, always the first to go home to bed, decided to have another rum instead.

Ray said, "Are you sure you can handle *two* drinks, Lyle?"

And Lyle said menacingly, "Strike up a tune, minstrel."

We sang a few more songs. We were waiting to see what would happen. For a long time nothing did. We played "It's Only a Shanty in Old Shanty Town," "Hey, Good Lookin'," and "Has Anybody Seen My Gal." I don't say it had anything to do with the particular song, but when we started in on "Rufus Blossom," who "had a head like a big sledge hammer / mouth like a terrible scar / but no one could touch him in Alabama / when he played on his old guitar . . ." Lyle came out of his seat as if he'd been catapulted. He said, "That sure puts rabbits in your feet, don't it?" and he took my sister by the hand and they clogged around the room a couple of times together. When the song was over she gave him a big hug and he sat down in his chair with an expression like he'd been shot between the eyes.

We just went along into something slower so we could keep an eye on Lyle. We knew as it happened we were witnessing an event we'd be talking about for the rest of our lives. Lyle had astonished himself more than anyone. He was looking straight ahead, not tapping his foot or anything. Then he reached under his chair and put his hat on real square and tight, stood up, strode to the door, turned toward my father and touched his brim and was gone. I guess he figured that was one thing in life he'd got done and didn't have to mess with again.

The next day he blamed me for getting him drunk. He said he'd lain in bed all night unable to sleep, his heart was pounding so loud.

Lyle wakes at two in the morning, not sure whether to blame his shortness of breath or the usual fidgets he gets in the middle of the night. He fits the oxygen mask over his face and lies back down and just breathes a little, then takes it off. It's the last tank, and as deep as the snow is now, and as young as April is, he may not get to town for a month or more. Maybe Bert will bring up a tank on the snowmobile when he comes, if the snow isn't too soft and he doesn't have to come on skis.

Lyle knows this feeling well enough not to fight it. He gets out of bed, holding his hernia in with one finger. He opens the draft on the stove a finger's width. He sits down in the easy chair and turns on the radio. He listens to what's coming in, the all-night truckers' station, as he rolls a cigarette. It's a station out of Oklahoma City that lists the road conditions across the nation. By determining what the interstates are like in California, Oregon, Nevada, and Utah, Lyle can get a better idea of what he's in for than he gets from the local weather predictions. Maybe if the roads are dry between here and the Sierras, and if it's not too cold on the northern border he can get some sleep.

No such luck. It's raining like hell from San Francisco to Point Arena. The sunshine that will be here tomorrow, courtesy of high pressure over the desert, will be overwhelmed by a severe winter storm the next day.

Paul Harvey says the National Weather Service, with all their satellites, balloons, computers, and color-coded maps, has a 60 percent accuracy rate. Sixty percent. That's 10 percent better than flipping a coin. November of 1974 they predicted light snow flurries and we got thirty-one inches in one night. I've heard them say sunshine when it was raining on the radio station.

183

Lyle doesn't like to say what he thinks will happen, but if you can get it out of him, he won't be wrong.

Once we were down haying, and over a break for a cigarette Lyle noted the stringy clouds that were making regular streaks in the upper atmosphere. He said, "Must be a hurricane shaping up in the Gulf." There was a hurricane brewing, but I never heard about it on the radio until about three days after Lyle had predicted it from observing the skies over Wyoming.

Lyle flicks the ash of his cigarette into the ashtray that is a beanbag on the bottom and an ashtray on the top, a brass arch rainbowing over the top with little half-circles bent into it to hold your cigarette when you put it down. Only Lyle never puts his down.

He rolls the dial to a talk show out of Denver, where people are holding forth on the problems divorcées have getting sex, and how important getting it is to their lives. One woman offers, "If I don't get sex at least once a week, I become violent with my children. I can't go out to the bars as much as I should because I can't afford a baby-sitter. Men don't want a woman who already has a brood weighing her down. What do you think I should do?"

Lyle is afraid he won't be able to stand the answer. He's predicting a different kind of weather. He says, "Jesus," and turns it off. He stubs out the last quarter of his smoke and rolls back into bed. He takes one more breath of oxygen and dozes off again till about four. He lies there doing nothing till five.

Then he gets up again and dresses in the dark and, with his workboots unlaced, shuffles into the kitchen. He sets a kerosene lamp on the counter and removes the glass chimney. He takes the lid-lifter off its nail and removes the forward lid over the firebox. He crumples a sheet of newspaper and drops it in. He throws in a handful of chips and splinters from around the chopping block, lights a match on the stove top, lights the lamp from it, then drops it onto the newspaper. Flames leap up like a faithful dog, illuminating Lyle's weather-drawn face as he peers into the firebox. He lays on two quarter-split pieces of lodgepole and throws back the draft that detours heat over to the oven for baking. He replaces the lid. The fire revs.

He throws another stick of wood on the fire and fills the tea kettle with water stored in an insulated tank, still steaming from circulating through the firebox in a copper coil the night before.

As the stove metal ticks, heating up, the sky brightens. Lyle puts his huge hand behind the lamp chimney and blows into his palm. The light's out. He goes to the cupboard and takes down a mixing bowl, opens the flour bin, and starts the batter for flapjacks.

It is light enough to see now, though no direct rays have struck the kitchen window by the time the pancakes are done. Lyle fries them one at a time and puts them in the warming oven. The last one he shovels out of the pan and lays on a separate dish on the shelf to cool. He stacks his own plate, pours the coffee, and sits down at the table. He looks out the south window over the white meadow.

In the last three years of his life, Ray began to manifest a strange relationship with snow. Sometimes in the fall or early winter, if he was on the mountain alone and Margie was in town, he'd flee to Laramie in a flat panic at the slightest suggestion of flurries. This in a man who was born on the mountain sixty-five years ago and had already seen everything this country can dish out and was well equipped to handle it: four-wheel drive with chains all around, a light two-cylinder snow cat with a cab, called a Trackster; and he always carried shovels, blankets, extra gasoline, and food. No way he could get into real trouble. Still, some nights, with light snow predicted and a few flakes in the air, I'd see Ray streaking by without so much as a wave, with a grim look on his face, headed for town.

On the other hand there were times—more than a few—when he'd get drunk as a barn swallow on old gooseberries in Laramie, and alone or with Ginny, his daughter, he'd head up here in the middle of the night in the worst whiteout you can imagine.

He'd load the Trackster, which was more than the pickup was designed to carry, and drive through the drifts like there were hellhounds after him, as if sheer momentum could get him through anything. It got him through a lot, but it also left him high-centered in the middle of some huge snowdrifts. I know because I dug him, pulled him, or dug and pulled him out of scores of such drifts in those days. If no one was around to lend a hand, Ray seemed perfectly happy to dig himself out, even if it took several hours. If he knew he couldn't dig out or the truck broke down, he'd just unload the Trackster and away he'd go, rattling over the tops of wavelike drifts, commenting on the tooth-loosening shriek of the two-cycle motor by mumbling every so often, "Well, I guess it beats walking."

I didn't think it did beat walking, since the Trackster moved at about the same pace as walking and sounded like the inside of a beehive. You had to shout to be heard by the person sitting next to you.

Frank reported one such night: a couple of feet of snow down, blowing into deeper drifts, more predicted, and with the wind whipping it to a froth. It was February just before calving. Frank and Shirley had just turned off their light and climbed into bed for the last good sleep they expected for a while, when Ray's headlights swept across the bedroom wall. They didn't get out of bed, just lay there as the truck idled in the yard. Once they heard Ginny laugh and it sounded like she'd had more than a few. One just assumed that by that time of night Ray was loose.

Frank peeked out the window. He could see the ends of two cigarettes glowing in the cab of the pickup. Snow swirled in the headlights like white mosquitoes. When he lay back down Frank said, "Nice evening for a drive in the country." Shirley giggled. Then the truck pulled up the hill past the house, and they went to sleep. Frank wondered how far they'd get, but he wasn't worried about them.

At midnight they woke again to a drunken whoop of laughter and, looking out the window, saw Ray pulling down the ramps to unload the Trackster. It was still coming down like hell. The thought of starting out on the seven miles to the reservoir at this hour in these conditions seemed less like drunk than crazy, but once the whine of the Trackster had faded into the blizzard, Frank just rolled over and went back to sleep. He noticed Shirley had beat him to it. His last conscious thought was, "I wonder how far they'll get this time."

It was sometime after two when Frank heard that overgrown chainsaw pull back into the ranch yard. When the throttle cut to idle he heard more laughter. At least they were having fun.

On the open ridges that anchor Boulder Ridge to the prairie, the snowdrifts resemble each other, and in the pitch black and white of a blizzard at night, they'd driven in circles for a couple of hours before Ginny convinced Ray to give it up after he said for the tenth time, "Oh, now I know where I am."

They came back to the ranch, loaded the Trackster, started the pickup, and backed it straight into a big irrigation ditch.

Frank kept checking out the window every so often and going back to bed. When they unloaded the Trackster again, he figured they were sure as hell stuck, the truck resting on its axles. When they started trying to pull the truck out of the ditch with the Trackster, Frank realized the moment he had dreaded had arrived.

It was three-thirty. He told Shirley to stay in bed. He pulled on his blue jeans, laced up his Sorels, put on his down coat and Scotch cap, and headed out to the barn to start the big tractor.

When Ray saw Frank he said he sure hadn't meant to get him out of bed. Frank was good-natured about it since he thought it was funnier than anything else, a funny story. With the big tractor and the nylon towrope, Frank still had to take a pretty good run at it to yank Ray's truck out of the snow-filled ditch.

Frank waited while they loaded the Trackster again and left. Then he went to bed for the hour or so before he would be getting up anyway. He lay there thinking about Ray and that crazy daughter of his plowing through the deeply rutted snow on the county road back to town, still passing a bottle. If Ray managed to keep it on the road he'd be back in Laramie by first light.

Besides the big hay barn at the end of the meadow (that used to be the meadow's waist before they built the reservoir), there was another barn in the brome patch behind the house. It was built at the same time or before the hay barn, on soft ground and without a real foundation, just rocked up at the corners and at the middle of each wall, so that it sank and the bottom logs rotted one by one until the peak of the roof was eye level. It sank about an inch a year. The earth was inhaling it.

You could scarcely store a small tractor in there, let alone hay or stock. Someday it will be a roof resting on the ground. Lyle knew there would have to be a new barn, and he kept it in the back of his mind when he did other things. When he was cutting firewood and found a straight, standing-dead building log the right size, he'd skid it home. He gathered logs ten years for that barn and never felled a living tree.

He knew it would be his last big job, so he made it monumental. The floor plan was twenty-four by forty feet; the logs were too big for a man to lift one end without block and tackle. He decided, again, against nails except for the roof. He decided to build it in winter.

I have never heard of anyone building a barn that size, alone, at that elevation, in the winter. In ambition it was like the first ascent of a great north face, though it was never reported in journals. Tourists can see the barn from the county road, but the accomplishment of its building was only known to about twenty people, fifteen of whom have died.

Before the snow flew Lyle hauled foundation stone from Bull Mountain, big square pieces weighing up to five hundred pounds. He built a boom on the REO and winched them up on the hand winch he'd made for sawlogs. He stacked and leveled them at the corners and where the logs joined at the middles of the long sides.

The previous winter he had forged two auger bits, one and a quarter inches in diameter, eighteen inches long, the kind of tool you couldn't buy anywhere. He made a special brace with an extra long sweep to turn his huge bits.

He worked in blizzards, alone, maneuvering the logs up onto the wall one end at a time, holding them temporarily with log dogs he'd also forged. With handsaw and double-bitted axe he fitted the corners, plumb and square, rolling the logs back again and again to trim a finer fit. You'd need a feeler gauge to check the tolerances. Each time he went up a log he augered clear through two logs and into the third, till the brace had buried itself. He trimmed pegs out of lodgepole sticks with the axe, and filled the walls so full of pegs it looked like a jail in some places. He went to one-inch pegs to fasten down the hand-hewn rafters.

Unless the wind was strong enough to blow him off the walls, or the logs were so iced he couldn't balance on them holding a twice-sharpened axe, he was out there. By the time the snow was gone the roof was on. All that remained was pouring the foundation.

Lyle always put the foundation in last, so the building can settle before it's tied down. If you rock the corners and start building you can use the bottom logs to hold the forms and pour the walls under them, so that the liquid cement takes the cupped shape of the logs, which have pegs sticking downward to tie them to the concrete, which makes a stronger, tighter fit than doing it "the right way."

Lyle's cement mixer was a 1923 Deere utility motor geared into a Model-T axle that turned a fifty-five-gallon drum that had wooden fins inside it. It mixed a wheelbarrow about as often as one man working alone can hand pour that much and get back. The few days I made it over that winter, Lyle let me help on things that would have been hard to screw up. I drilled holes, and later helped shovel sand out of the creek for cement.

I watched Lyle hewing with the broadaxe, saw him cut the perfect corners with stunningly confident strokes of the double-bitted axe. I can walk into that barn today and look up into the massive vaults of rafters, cross beams, struts, and remember. I can look around and know one thing at least is for damn sure *there*.

From 1948 to 1972 Bill McMurray never worked a lick over what he had to, mostly reading clocks and turning the wheels that open the gate on the reservoir and the headgates on the ditches. At first he had to snowshoe nine miles up to Deadman during heavy runoff season, but as soon as they invented the snowmobile, Bill got one, and why not. He had tried to make the snowshoe trip up there and back easier by nailing a crosspiece between two trees for a bench every quarter mile so he could sit down and rest without having to take off his pack or snowshoes. Bill must have thought there would be the same amount of snow every year; some winters the rests are under the snow, other years they're eye-level or overhead. That was Bill.

Most of the time he spent drinking beer in front of the TV hooked up to a twelve-volt battery. His wife was not pretty, but she was kind. Her name was Elbertine. Elbertine and everyone else cut Bill a lot of slack, even his employers who suspected they'd have a hard time finding someone else to live that far from town, even with fringe benefits like letting him run cows on the section and pocket the proceeds.

Bill didn't care much for fixing fence. Theoretically he was responsible for half his north side (our south), and half his east side (Lyle's west), and all of his fence that bordered National Forest or railroad land. Bill never worked on our side, and we stopped expecting him to. We fixed it ourselves each spring.

The half of Bill's east fence got so bad it didn't need to be fixed anymore; it needed to be rebuilt: new posts and new wire which the company would provide, but mostly it required a few postholes, which Bill was supposed to provide. Since the cows arrived in early June, and pasture rent was real money for Bill, Lyle expected him to get after it eventually—greed kept Bill from being completely lazy.

As soon as the snowdrifts released the worst parts, Lyle went to work on his fence. Before the snow was all the way gone Lyle's fencing was done and he was waiting on Bill to fix his part. Lyle talked to him about it a couple of times, "mentioned it," more likely: the western politesse of obliqueness. He secured assurances, pats on the back, chuckles, good-neighbor smiles. The first of June came and the fence just lay there like a strafed parade.

Lyle decided to fight the unthinkable with the unthinkable. He drove to Bill and Elbertine's to speak of the fence directly, to make demands. Bill and Elbertine had gone to town.

Lyle went home and loaded the pickup with posts he'd cut and treated himself, fencing tools, and a new roll of wire. He set to work building fence, and with every post he set he got madder at Bill. He'd started at nine in the morning and was still working at seven, when Bill drove up in his company truck.

He was all duded up for town and had Elbertine and Elbertine's sister with him. He stopped right next to the posthole Lyle was digging, then calm as you please rolled down the window. He didn't even get out of his truck, just gave Lyle a big grin, easy as thought, and asked how the fence was coming. "How's the fence coming, Lyle?"

Lyle dropped the shovel into the hole and turned around. He had never uttered an emphatically negative word to anyone's face in his life. Generally, there's no style in it. Lyle lit into Bill with volume and purpose, chewed him up one side and down the other, calling him a lazy, good-for-nothing stump not worth the powder to blow it to hell sitting there in his goddamned string tie and town duds, letting another man do his work for him. It was shameful and he was a sorry excuse for a man if there ever was one. Lyle deployed words he ordinarily wouldn't have, in front of ladies.

Elbertine kept saying, "That's right. You tell him, Lyle. I tell him that all the time, but it don't do no good. Like talking to a worm." When it looked to Bill like the storm wasn't going to let up, he just let that grin slip a notch and reached for the window crank. Bill kept smiling, rolled up the window, easy as thought, and drove away.

Lyle turned back to work in the gathering dark. He decided that building fence was bad enough; building it mad just wasn't worth it.

The next time he saw Bill it was like nothing had happened. The cows grazed peacefully, the men were friendly, and they had a new fence between them.

I never knew Howard very well, and what I knew I couldn't figure. I'll never know why Ray took him on that last trip up the mountain in a snowstorm, unless it was because Ray didn't mind the idea of being dead, he just didn't like the idea of being dead a long time before anyone found him. That was a lonesome idea. It never occurred to Ray that Howard wouldn't make it out. Howard was supposed to have gotten out with word.

To meet Howard you'd have thought him pretty normal: a short, bearded fellow, perhaps overeager to please. You had to be around him some to realize that he was without volition to the point of dementia. He did what he was told, but he never did anything else. Ray said Howard had an older brother he just about had to check with before taking a piss. That's why it got our attention when Howard married Nita, Jack's daughter, who, like Kye, Jack's son, was afflicted with a degenerative illness that made them obese, mentally defective, and eventually blind. Kye and Nita were utterly gentle. They belonged to that elite society of people who, because defective in a certain way, go through life without hurting anyone. They were enormous, blind child angels.

Howard worshiped "Uncle Ray," and mimicked his boozing and whatever words and gestures he could affect. He was tickled to death when Ray asked him to go up the mountain.

They loaded the Trackster and headed for the reservoir in a March snowstorm. At least it was daylight. They drove as far as the abandoned Running Water buildings, where, Frank later said, it looked like they'd gotten stuck, dug out, and decided to go by Trackster from there. It was probably dark by the time they reached my house. No one was home but Ray had a key. I know they stopped in because I found one of Ray's Parliaments with the filter bitten the way Ray did. It was in the ashtray, just the one, meaning they didn't stay long. They headed up toward the ridge to follow it to the reservoir, probably very drunk by then.

It wasn't unusual in those days for Ray to lose the road and head off in some screwy direction. His tracks were sometimes laughably astray. He headed off the road where it climbs straight up the side of the ridge and ended up in the trees, in the deep spring powder. The Trackster foundered, and when Ray revved it up it just dug a hole for itself.

So far, though, nothing was unusual. Why they didn't walk back the half-mile of packed track to my house, where they knew there was wood and food for exactly such an occasion, I'll never know. Nor will I know why Ray, who kept blankets, food, and two five-gallon cans of extra gasoline in the Trackster for exactly such an occasion, had apparently forgotten all these things.

So they sat there, keeping the Trackster running for its heater till it ran out of gas. They passed the bottle and smoked cigarettes. They had left the shovels locked in the cab of the pickup, four miles back.

When spring came I found a few charred pine twigs with which Howard must have tried to start a fire. They had no snowshoes; they couldn't gather dry wood.

Frank said Howard must have gone back to the pickup for the shovels, but when he got there, he didn't have the keys. He started back to Ray for the keys, but drunk, out of shape, and underdressed, he didn't make it. Frank found Howard's body about a quarter-mile from the Trackster, face down in the snow.

Since it wasn't unusual for Ray to get snowed in for a week, and since there was no telephone, Margie never worried until the following Sunday, when the weather was clear and the boys didn't come down.

No one knew whether Ray should be looked for in Albany County, Wyoming, or Larimer County, Colorado. Both counties refused to send rescue parties until they knew for sure where Ray was lost.

Frank went up on his snowmobile and found them, in Colorado. Then the sheriff's rescue team came with snow machines, helicopters, and walkie-talkies.

Freezing to death is supposed to be relatively painless, especially if you're drunk. Frank said Ray was frozen solid. He must have gotten out to take a piss and tipped over backward, since his pants were unzipped and he was out. The posse had to be careful not to break it off. Ray must have liked the tickle of snowflakes on his face because Frank said he was smiling.

Drunk, lying on his back in the deep, soft snow, looking up into the gently falling sky, smiling. For ten days the storm buried him and uncovered him and buried him and uncovered him like it was looking at something.

Between the dead gray tree standing in the forest and the tree of smoke that resurrects itself from the chimney, each piece of wood is handled six times: hauled out of the timber in logs, unloaded, cut to length on a tractor-powered buzz saw, stacked, put in the woodbox, put in the stove; seven times if you have to split it. Lyle had a woodpile the size of a schoolhouse, enough fuel for two or more years. If he got hurt and couldn't cut wood some year, he wouldn't have to depend on anyone else, and he still wouldn't freeze.

Lyle added to the woodpile every year. It got so old and big the bottom pieces began to rot and the wooden mountain began leaning and had to be propped. Lyle kept adding to it each year, a little more than he burned in a year, and the woodpile loomed.

Ray questioned the practicality of cutting new wood every year when perfectly good fuel was rotting in the pile. Lyle said, "I ain't about to restack it, and besides, if I build it up it works like a snowfence, keeps snow off the house."

Emphysema began to erode Lyle's health. Digging out the woodpile was no longer a welcome bit of exercise in a snowbound winter; it was a potentially fatal necessity. Loading and hauling furnace wood to the house on a sledge was bad enough—shoveling out the woodpile was likely to kill him. He needed a woodshed.

Lyle figured he could still get in a year's supply of wood if he took all summer doing it. When I offered to put up his wood for him he said, "Goddammit, there's just a few things I can still do for myself around this place, and I don't want you taking them." The real problem was shoveling snow.

Lyle had never built a woodshed because it was too easy, beneath his interest as a craftsman. Now he needed to build one to stay alive. By then Lyle couldn't drive a nail without resting before it was all the way in. I helped him as much as he would let me. He appreciated the help, but he resented it, too. Once or twice he was pretty short with me, and I already felt as if everything I did, every lick, was substandard compared to how Lyle would have done it.

He cut and dragged in all the poles he needed. I dug the holes and set the treated uprights. Together we lifted and fit the cross beams, drilled and bolted them. When it came to covering the walls, Lyle wanted to cut and nail all the boards himself. He had some one-by-twelves he'd milled about thirty years ago. He'd saw halfway through a plank then sit down on the sawhorse and suck air for five minutes. He took all day to nail on a dozen boards.

I hewed the rafters, which irked Lyle—by then he was taking it like medicine. We set them and trimmed them together. He had salvaged some Strongbarn roofing and insisted on nailing it up himself. Again I was sent away. When I came back the next week the roof was done. He'd put a skylight in. He was busy hanging doors.

He built the woodshed over as much of the woodpile as would fit in it, so he didn't have to move it. He never cut firewood again. He started burning that rotten wood he'd cut as much as forty years ago, when he still had a family to keep warm. One day he paused over the cookstove with the lid-lifter in his hand and said, "You know, there's more heat in that old rotten wood than you'd think."

W hat the hell is that?"
"A saw."
"What kind of saw?"
"For cutting out a wooden wheel. It cuts a perfect circle."
"What do you want to make a wooden wheel for?"
"A wheelbarrow."
I knew better than to ask why Lyle didn't just slide down to the True Value and get himself one with a nice rubber wheel.

The saw was like a big hardwood picture frame, only the sides were all turned out fancy on the lathe, and there was a piece of bandsaw blade stretched across its middle. It was just like Lyle to spend a week or more building a tool he would only use once.

I wondered how you get the spokes all in between the hub and rim. Lyle showed me a piece of fir he'd found that had just the right curve for a handle. He only had one, though, so it was like the pistol grips all over again: He had to scour the timber for the piece that matched it.

After dinner we went for a walk in the woods. Lyle studied each tree we passed, searching for the handle's mate. I was supposedly helping, but I wouldn't have opened my mouth had I seen a piece that looked close. I knew Lyle wasn't missing anything. I pretended to be looking, to know what I was looking for, but really I was just trailing along like a pup.

We didn't find the right piece that day, but Lyle found it later and shaved them down to match with a draw-knife. Each handle was also half the frame the box was mounted on, so they were long, about six feet, straight where they made the frame, then sweeping up and back to become the grips.

He cut out, mounted, and trued the wheel, and forged a steel rim. He got bearings from the junkheap and balanced the box just right. He knew his strength was going, and he thought a big wheelbarrow might make things easier around the place. It might help him stay there longer.

A fellow brought Lyle a ruined treadle grindstone rotted off its frame. Building a new frame for that grindstone and trueing it up was the other project Lyle had going that summer. Lyle didn't need a grindstone; he had three or four. The project was to keep a beautiful stone from becoming a lawn decoration, or worse.

He hunted up a couple of bearings, and just to make sure no one would ever have to do that job again, he welded a steel frame for it, and mounted an old tractor seat to it for extra comfort while pumping the treadle that turned the wheel. With good bearings and a true stone (the heavier the better), with the right leverage on the armature, it takes about as much effort to turn a grindstone with footpower as it does to scratch your ear.

Lyle had to build a tripod to lift the stone onto its frame. Once mounted he turned it slowly, and with a small cold chisel he pocked the stone to balance it. Then he turned the wheel fast and trued it with a high-carbon tool bit. It took two weeks of turning to make the wheel true.

It was clear that Lyle wasn't going far from his house anymore, unless it was to town, so as soon as the snow melted I went over on horseback to fix his fence. Pasturing cows was the only income Lyle had left. He qualified for social security but wouldn't take it because he had never paid into it. He never made enough money to file taxes either.

I pieced together the short lengths of wire that lay on the ground.

Scraps of cloth, tongues of worn-out work boots, bits of wire, buttons, bent nails, recipes, magazine articles, gunnysacks—Lyle never threw out anything that might someday have a use. He didn't have it in him. It was partly the result of being raised in poverty ("You never outgrow the way you grew up," he said), but I know Lyle thought of his own being the same way (like one of those boot tongues or scraps of wire). He thought, someday, probably after he died, his own purpose might finally be revealed to him.

I know because he told me.

After he died the auctioneers went through everything. The contents of his house that were considered valueless were emptied into eighty-five black plastic bags that lined the walk, like a bile the house spewed out.

They were loaded into Eddie's horse trailer and hauled away to the dump.

LYLE, 1980

"Did you know that the first line in Hamlet is the same, outside of not being in Spanish, as Billy the Kid's last words? Well, it is."

I have some snapshots of Lyle sitting at his kitchen table. He was baking bread that day, using his mother's recipe. The prints are glossy, high contrast. Lyle looks like a Vermeer under many coats of varnish. His face is long, lantern-jawed. He has a thin nose and a wide mouth. He looks aristocratic. The lines grooved into his face are angular, especially around his eyes and the folds of skin hooding his eyes, as if from a lifetime of squinting into snowglare. His eyes are pale blue and so piercing, that even from a photo he seems to be looking around inside you. He's balding. He's smiling. Everything he's ever done, or seen, or felt, or thought is brought to bear on his expression. He's sort of smiling.

Clara's diary contains an entry concerning a moonshine cabin they went looking for above Sheep Creek by Slickrock. Bill had run into an old-timer in town, a fellow with a long white beard who seemed to know the country, who claimed there was a moonshine cabin tucked into a ravine near Slickrock. Bill didn't want to climb up any gullies or draws or sidehills, so Clara, Lyle, and Elbertine went looking for it while Bill fished in Sheep Creek.

The diary entry doesn't mention anything about finding the moonshine cabin. They didn't. It aggravated Lyle that there was a whole house up there that he, who could find geodes and crystals, agates and arrowheads, and game in lean years, couldn't find.

So he went back in winter on snowshoes, searched all the same ravines and springs, went halfway to Deadman, looking. Nothing.

Coming down it began to blizzard. It was a crazy swirl that would hide your fingers from you and then lift so you could go a bit, and then it would come down again. Once the snow lifted just in time for Lyle to see that he was walking off a cliff. It was sixty feet straight down into a side drainage just above Sheep Creek. Lyle followed the edge downstream. The snow blew in, then lifted, blew in and lifted. Something caught his eye, some manmade form on the far side of the canyon, a square shape and an oblong one. It was the door and window of a cabin, built halfway up the far escarpment, under an overhang. Then the blizzard closed down for good and Lyle considered himself lucky to find home.

Lyle went back the next summer, thinking to enter that

cabin and see what was there. He found what he was certain was the right drainage; he found what he was certain was the overhang the cabin was built under. There was no cabin there. Lyle muttered, "It mighta been here but it's gone now."

My dad was headed downcountry Christmas Eve, riding the front of a storm. All the children were grown and gone, and he was spending Christmas with a friend in Denver. There were a couple of feet of powder down, and more in the air and more on the way, but with four-wheel drive and chains on all fours he was making it out all right.

When he reached the abandoned Running Water Ranch he thought he was hallucinating. Riding up through the ghostly, winterbound cabins and barns was a figure in the swirling snow. When he saw my father the rider turned his mount and headed over. Dad said later it was like a Frederic Remington painting come to life. The horse was big and had a thick sorrel coat. The rider was wearing shoepacks with spurs, sheepskin chaps, a Scotch cap with a scarf tied around it. He was wrapped in a heavy woolen blanket. The stock of a Model '94 Winchester protruded from a saddle scabbard.

When the rider stopped my father was struck by the youthful, clean-shaven face. It was Clay.

"Are you lost?"

"Probably."

"What brings you out on this fine day?"

"Thought I'd ride over and invite Lyle to Christmas dinner with us. Didn't think the snowmobile would make it through the drifts between your place and his. Nothing stops this nag."

"Do you think Lyle will come down for dinner?"

"Oh, I know for a fact he won't, but we ask him every year, just so he knows he can if he wants."

"And you're riding fifteen miles through deep snow in a blizzard to invite Lyle to a dinner you are sure he won't attend?"

Clay looked down at his horse as if he'd never seen one before. "Looks like it."

It was the summer I memorized Lyle's huge hands gripping the oaken steering wheel of the 1930 REO flatbed. I was doing that because it was the first summer Lyle couldn't buck bales anymore, and I knew I wouldn't be haying many more times, not with Lyle anyway, and not on this meadow. Emphysema was chipping away at his independence.

The baler kept missing ties. It rained every afternoon. Lyle pinched a nerve in his neck from driving forward looking back, mowing, raking, baling, over and over the same ground he'd gone over and over for forty years. Ray convinced Lyle to see a chiropractor in Fort Collins. Lyle wouldn't have gone if there hadn't been hay to cut and he hadn't been nearly paralyzed with pain and muscle spasms in his neck, shoulder, and arm. The problem was, the drive home following the treatments left him in worse shape than he'd started in, so he quit going.

Out of denim strips he sewed a harness that fit under his chin and behind the back of his head; it joined on the top, where he sewed a loop. He screwed an eye hook into the ceiling above his chair, and ran a nylon string from the head harness up through the eye hook, and suspended a bucket with five pounds of salt in it from the other end of the string. He sat in the chair and hung his head from the ceiling for four days until he'd fixed the pinched nerve. Just like fixing any mechanism—easier than most. Then he went back to work and finished haying.

We hayed the next year as well, me doing all the loading and stacking, Lyle still driving the tractors, but the summer before the last one was the summer I memorized his hands.

When the Van Wanings moved to Sheep Creek they were resigned to being snowed in. In 1940 everyone around here was. But down in that valley, and as far back in the timber as they settled, they were more snowed in than anyone.

From the start Lyle parked his pickup over at Pat Sudeck's for the winter, a mile and a half away. If the road across the prairie was blown clear and the timber drifted under, Lyle could snowshoe over the hill and drive to town. That meant packing supplies on snowshoes. After ten years of it, sometimes making trips with a sledge, Lyle decided to invent a snow machine.

It was ten years before the first snowmobile appeared; it must have been one of those ideas in the air at a certain time. Lyle built his snow machine on a wooden frame, with wood skis and a wooden track with rubber cleats cut out of old tires. It was powered by a 1923 single-cylinder Deere utility motor (the same motor he used to power his cement mixer). The snow machine worked, but it was underpowered and the track kept tearing itself apart. After a certain point, snowshoeing took less time than fixing the machine, so he replaced its track with fixed runners. He left the skis in front and mounted a Chevrolet six where the Deere had been. He took a piece of quarter-sawn six-by-six from the lumber pile and disappeared into the shop to fashion an airplane propeller. For someone whose two brothers had been killed in airplanes it was a curious design choice. The fact is, though, an airpowered snow sled wouldn't tear itelf apart.

I don't know where he got specifications for the pitch of the prop blades, or how he made it balanced and symmetrical by hand. But a trial run in the meadow revealed an oversight: The sled wouldn't run at less than sixty miles an hour. Lyle was a streak across the blank expanse until he could shut it off, luckily before he went through the west fence.

He hung the propeller on the shop wall and waited for the rest of the world to invent the snow machine. Not long after, they did. Harry Benson loaned Lyle a used double-track, single-ski model that wasn't too fast, and it swam through drifts to the pickup truck for twenty-five winters.

So every winter Lyle left his truck parked at our place, out on a windthrashed knoll, staring down the barrel of every storm, snowdrifts breaking over it, the wind scooping, scalloping its shape free again.

Lyle left his truck just past where the timber ends and walked home in the fall, before the heavy snow. He walked back for it in the spring. All winter he ground over the hill, threading the winter road, in the chained-up Power Wagon, gearing down to churn like a stern-wheeler where it's deepest. During the worst snow he snowmobiled, skimming over the wavy drifts. If the snow was too deep or rotten to snowmobile on, he didn't go. Sometimes the prairie was snowbound as well. He didn't go.

It was the end of November. Lyle's health had been on the skids for two years or more. He had no wind and his heart was weak. Lyle checked the Thomson's Lumber thermometer mounted outside on the window trim: 10. It had snowed and was bound to storm again.

Two pairs of wool pants over long johns, Sorels, wool shirt, down coat, hat, gloves. He stepped out of the woodwarm mud porch and into the real air. He pulled the door to and locked it, thinking simultaneously, *No one is around*, and, *You never know who could be creeping around*.

The truck started instantly at full choke and purred at idle while Lyle rolled a smoke. The meadow looked like a white dinner plate with willows down its middle. He put the cigarette in the corner of his mouth, giving it a final twist. He fished the Zippo from his shirt pocket, tilted his head to avoid its six-inch flame, and flashed the end of his cigarette.

He pulled out into the yard to chain up. He had a block of cast concrete in the back of the truck for extra traction.

Going over the hill he had no problem. As he drove past the sidehill where the winter road attacks the ridge he just glared; he had fought that hill for forty winters. Every winter it rose white against him and he fought it, sidling down the sidehill into deeper drifts, digging out, grinding in again.

He parked the truck in the usual place, left the keys in the ashtray and the doors unlocked. Taking the truck over the hill marked a significant day in Lyle's year, not fixed on the calendar, but meaning more thereby, marking the beginning of his winter exile, recalling winters past, the best and the worst. He slammed the door and started walking home.

He could feel that the temperature had plummeted in the last few minutes. As soon as he set out he knew he had overestimated his strength. By the time he reached the first cattleguard he was running on disbelief: How could a two-mile stroll become a mortal threat?

The pace he'd started with was pushing it so he dropped it a notch. No one was watching him from the trees, but if they had been they would have thought him stock-still unless they watched for a long time.

He passed the spot where Ray froze to death before he was sure he was in trouble. Winded, he gasped aloud, "Hell, I ain't even drunk, Raymond." His lungs were searing. He was lightheaded. He thought, I'm almost as close to home as I am to the truck now, I'd just as well try to make it. Besides, if I went back now it would have been for nothing and I'd have to try again. I want this to be the last time I ever walk this hill.

When he reached the ridge, two hours after he'd begun, he sat down on a boulder cleared by wind and sun. He was gasping like a fish. His lungs were filling with liquid. He was drowning. The rest of the way was downhill, but he had no feeling in his hands or feet. The sweet release of giving up occurred to him, how easy it would be never to rise again, to harden and become crystalline, like a made thing, to freeze in sitting position until spring when someone would come along and find him, just resting.

The cold was to his knees and elbows, rising, but he was breathing better for resting, and he rose and started walking again, shuffling stiffly, unbearably slowly, pushing as fast as he could go. By the time the yellow Windcharger came in sight he was resting half a minute after each step, the way Himalayan climbers do. He still thought he might die in the yard; he had already fallen twice. He was delirious. Then his hand was on the doorhandle. The fire was out. It took a long time to start. He ate and drank nothing. By the time the house was warm it was dark. He still half-expected, half-wished to die. He knew how badly he'd run himself down. The next day his legs swelled to twice their normal size. The pickup was over the hill.

In 1949 Lyle's brother, Bob, had a hard time with horses. Mowing hay they spooked at a jackrabbit and took out about a hundred feet of fence. Bob was pretty thoroughly sanded down, not hurt bad anyplace, but hurt not bad everyplace. That same fall he and Lyle were skidding out sawlogs when the horses bolted and dragged Bob by the reins on a whirlwind tour of the forest floor. He broke a rib. That's why Lyle went to tractors, though anytime you are around turning gears and sickle bars you have to count your fingers pretty regularly. You have to *Pay Attention*. I don't have enough fingers to count the fellows I know who have lost some of theirs, mostly either from farm machinery or roping. Almost anything Lyle did was hazardous, and after his brothers were gone he mostly worked alone: felling trees with chainsaws; balancing on the top log of a barn; hewing with an axe so sharp that a couple of fingers or toes wouldn't even slow it down; or just out fencing—old wire can snap under the stretcher and come at you like a snake, or lay open the side of your face like a stiletto.

Just last week two kids were stringing fence on a ranch not far from here. They were working on a sidehill. They had a hundred yards or so of wire laid out on the ground, four strands. They were pulling the wire out of a spool mounted in the pickup bed. The wire lazed on the ground in loose spirals. The truck was parked, but it jumped out of gear and started rolling, gathering barbed wire into a raging snarl under the wheels and axles. Only one kid saw it. He tried to jump into the cab to step on the brakes and save the truck from augering into the ditch at the bottom of the hill. Here is what his friend saw: one pantleg got snagged by the wire before the boy could get the door open. He was

214

running alongside and then he was pulled underneath into the gathering, snapping rage of wire. The truck raised a little puff of dirt at the bottom of the ravine. There was nothing left of that kid bigger than a finger.

Lyle learned to pay attention, to think things through and not get ahead of himself, not to lapse into inattention ever. After a while he couldn't *not* pay attention, shaking a stranger's hand, tasting Mrs. So and So's pickles, setting fenceposts. It endowed all his actions with precision. It gave him total recall. It obliterated time.

Lyle never would have gone to the hospital if it hadn't been for the second hernia, which he got on his last trip to town loading his oxygen tanks. He said the first one hadn't bothered him much over the years. He sewed a denim truss, and whenever the thing popped out he just popped it back in, like when the REO popped out of second gear going downhill against the compression—just pop it back in. But this new hernia hurt and wouldn't go back in. He pushed on it and worked it around till he passed out. Then he put Anbesol on it and pushed on it some more. It was Clay who finally convinced Lyle to go to the hospital for a "tune up." Lyle figured then he could come home and die of what was really killing him.

"I better die soon," he said. "If I don't I'll have to move away. I can't make another winter here. I sure don't want to move. Don't think I could do it. All I ever wanted to be was home."

We loaded him into the back of the station wagon. He didn't even glance at the meadow before he got in. He lay down beside his oxygen tank, his new, ugly bride. He had some delirium. He said, picking at the air near his knee, "I've gotten into this habit I have to quit. I keep seeing something there and I try to grab it, but I can't." Then he said, "Jim, the next pickup I buy is going to be an automatic."

He died the second night, in his sleep. A nurse said, "Who was that old man? In here two days and nights and he never asked for a thing. You could dust that call button for finger prints and he'd be innocent."

A couple of weeks before he died Lyle made a drawing for my daughter, Emily. He'd seen a cloud over the meadow that looked like a dinosaur and drew a picture of it. Lyle called it "Cloudosaurus."

217

I was having coffee with Bert and his wife, Joyce, in Laramie. The mortuary (which prefers to be called the funeral home) called: "Do you want the coffin open or closed?" Joyce turns to me with the phone in her hand. "Do we want the coffin open or closed?" I thought about it. "I don't think Lyle would have had any particular interest in being seen dead. Closed."

"Do you want cremation or embalming?"

"Jesus, I don't know. I think Don Ruth is the one Lyle told all this stuff to, and he's on a pack trip. I guess we better embalm him until we find out, then we can still cremate him if that's what he wanted. You can't do it the other way 'round."

"Okay. They say he needs some clothes. You brought him in in his underwear and they can't put him in the coffin like that."

"Why not, if it's closed?"

"They say it's a law. They say he needs some clothes this afternoon."

"That means I have to drive an hour up there, rummage around in Lyle's closet for that 1930s suit he has. Then I have to drive it back here and then drive home. It'd be easier for me to give Lyle the clothes I'm wearing now and just drive home naked."

Bert said, "I think I have an old suit I can take over there."

"Bless you."

The coffin looked like a birthday cake, flocked pink. We had ordered it by phone. I knew Lyle would have ordered the cheapest for himself, so I ordered the second cheapest, which turned out to be far and away the tackiest. It looked like it was designed for family pets. It was piñata-esque. I figured Lyle could only see it from the inside.

Luckily Mac McCartney had cut some pine boughs on Boulder Ridge, and we were pretty well able to hide the coffin. Everyone who'd known Lyle was there. The three half-sisters Lyle had hardly known but willed his meadow to wept.

The preacher was the nondenominational one in town, and, indeed, he is a nondenominational kind of guy, mild and grayish. He says funeral services for all the folks who die who don't belong to a particular church. Many he doesn't know personally, which was his relationship with Lyle. He basically paraphrased the obituary in reverse order, and wrenched from that text three or four occasions to turn our thoughts toward Jesus. It was thin soup. He concluded he would have liked Lyle, had he known him, because the obituary had made him sound so "interesting."

I thought Lyle wouldn't mind that any more than the coffin. The guy was just doing his job. All who knew Lyle held their peace, their grief, their memories, their reverence.

After the service there was coffee at Bert and Joyce's house. The three half-sisters repaired to the sun porch with a realtor. We could not hear what they were saying, but we could see them through the glass, as if they were in an aquarium. There were muffled cries.

They ironed things out right then and there, while Carl talked cattle business with Clay, Jorie talked with Shirley and June, and Ruby held forth to the astonished company about how she eavesdrops on the radio-phone and the kind of dirt she hears. It's the next best thing to daytime TV, especially now that she's blind from diabetes, and the radio-phone has the added attraction that she actually *knows* a lot of the people talking. Sometimes she even interrupts the conversations of strangers with what she considers to be essential pertinencies.

Vi, one of the half-sisters, approached Joyce. "Lyle must have been quite a wealthy man. We had no idea."

"What makes you think he was wealthy?"

"Well, last night we went to the Home to view the body. I know it was supposed to be closed casket, but I'd never seen him. We were just curious as to what he looked like. Well. He must have had more money than we thought. He was wearing a Brooks Brothers suit."

Joyce said, "You looked at the label?"

"Mmm-hmmm."

All conversations were cut off mid-sentence when Joyce raised her voice to a shrill pitch, "Bert, you son of a bitch. You buried that old man in the suit you married me in. What the hell does that mean?"

The morning of the actual interment in Fort Collins we drove to Lyle's ranch to get his hat. There were a dozen or so wild irises about to bloom in the yard. For years we had brought Lyle irises from Tie Siding because they wouldn't grow this high, not even in the meadow. Here they were, about to bloom, though I suspect they would have winter-killed if left there. We spaded up a bunch of them and put them in a cardboard box with plenty of native soil to plant on Lyle's grave.

At the cemetery my five-year-old daughter put Lyle's old felt hat on top of the coffin. Jorie said a little poem about a blacksmith laying down his hammer at last. That was it. We went home. Boulder Ridge, Lyle's meadow, Lyle gone.

Lyle told me he could hear different tones emitted by different stars on the stillest, coldest winter nights. He said he could tell which notes came from which stars. He couldn't hear them all the time, just winter nights, and then, when he was about sixty, he admitted sadly that he couldn't hear them anymore. Age, I guess. When he said he heard the stars, though, he wasn't exaggerating. In fact, he was worried I'd think he was nuts, even though he knew I had never in thirty-five years heard him say anything but the absolute truth as far as he knew it. If Lyle said he heard stars he heard stars. The only reason he mentioned it was because it was curious to him, the idea of the music of the spheres and all.

Another time, while sorting through a fruitcake tin filled with old buttons, he told me how once in winter he was walking in deep timber with his axe. He heard a wind coming up, firing the treetops. He heard it getting closer. It reached the trees directly overhead. As it rushed into them Lyle felt the wind blow through him, blowing right through him as if he wasn't there.

I'm thinking of Lyle making a pair of silver and agate earrings with no girl in mind to give them to.

The sky was not blue all summer, nor did it rain. Sunsets were bloody without clouds. Half the west was on fire and no way to stop it in the driest summer in recorded history. The timber not already ablaze was sunsoaked to the point, it seemed, of spontaneous ignition. You couldn't see the mountains for smoke. Four thousand acres of timber burned not eight miles from us, and smoke from the Yellowstone fire four hundred miles away covered our state. There was a grass fire that barely sidled by us.

At the same time the land was being brutalized by fire and drought, we saw more wildlife than ever before: bear, puma, snowy egrets.

Waiting for winter to stop the fires, we started feeling better when the meadow wore a slip of frost through the morning. There was something reassuring about the meadow under snow, but then I thought of Lyle's empty kitchen up there some midwinter night: no light, no fire, rooms colder than the outside air, cold moonlight on the cold iron of the Majesty kitchen stove—no one looking out the window at the meadow, luminous in her snowy bed, a sleeping princess who doesn't care for waking.

People who didn't know Lyle well considered him moody. Ed Wilkes wouldn't sit down when he first came in, until he'd tested Lyle's mood. If Lyle's mood was good, Ed'd sit and visit. If not, he'd just leave. No sense in getting chewed on by some pissed hermit. Those of us who'd known Lyle longer knew he didn't have moods, he had weather. Not some inner weather that could have been a mood—Lyle had *the* weather. Inside him he had going on exactly what was going on in the sky, or some combination of recent weather and what was likely to develop. Old friends were perfectly happy to sit down and get snowed on for a couple of hours over coffee, though anyone would have preferred the happy emanations of cloudless sky and sun, even if the sun was shining on a snowdrift ten feet deep.

That high in the mountains a man lives less on the land than in the sky. After forty years the weather had all the bearing. It's like the drive train in a car, going through the differential and turning the wheels.

Oh, I know everyone's moods are affected by weather, but with no one around to put him in a mood, and his own actions honed down to rightness, Lyle just had straight weather inside and out.

It takes a lot of weather to make a winter bad, whereas a couple of weeks in summer, with the east wind dug in, cold vapor shifting in the meadow, the garden's fenceposts and the timbered ridges hard to make out except for dreamy glimpses, could generate as much gloom as being snowed in for a month. A week of wind could make him edgy as a civet cat. A piddle of useless thundershower on cut hay could make him almost cynical. But when the sun shone and the air was mild, a cheerfulness that had no source in his circumstance or prognosis emanated from his soul. A January thaw made him transcendently cheerful, though tobacco smoke had opened its black cloak inside him and he knew it. He could be happy snowed in and dying alone, if only the sun kept shining.

We say the meadow is in clouds when really clouds are in the meadow. We say steam rises out of the creek like it's turning its soul loose turning inside out and it is. Dew has neglected not a single leaf or blade of grass of all the millions. The fenceposts past the garden disappear again. We can't start haying till the sky returns. Lyle sits in the kitchen by the window not smoking, not reading, not drinking coffee. This morning he woke without the heart even to go out to the shop and get after some useless project, like those earrings. He is concentrating hard on just sitting, trying to shoo his mind away from the regions of memory and despair. He is waiting for the weather to change and it won't and he is waiting.

Who wouldn't want to die in good weather, instead of some mood?

Lyle's last winter was too mean to die in, though it would have been easier to die then. Five months he couldn't get to town. Bert hauled oxygen tanks by snowmobile; Ed and Toya brought groceries in the company's new Trackster. The gasoline power plant quit and Lyle didn't have the strength to snowshoe out to the Windcharger to turn it on. He went back to kerosene lights, and with the water pump out, he bathed in a washtub with water heated on the woodstove, the old way, the way they did forty-five years ago. The shape his body was in told him something had happened in all that time.

He hung on till summer took a good hold. June sun sponged into the pale aspen leaves. He wasn't getting out of bed anymore. We only figured out later he had cut off his intake of food, liquids, and medication. Jorie was housecleaning for him—he hadn't cleaned all winter and it was depressing. As she dusted, careful to replace exactly each object, she tried to keep up a cheerful chatter of news and questions.

Lyle said, "Hand me that box"—the one she was putting back after dusting the bureau. She handed it to him. He turned it over, studying it. He handed it back. "Ain't that pretty?"

Jorie sat down in an overstuffed chair that was bathed in windowlight. She looked at the box, one Lyle had made. He had carved it from a single block of apple wood so that with the lid on all the grain lined up and made its two-partedness disappear. The sides of the box were as thin as the sides of a violin. It was finished simply, with oil. On the lid were carved three cattails among cattail leaves, all gently bending.

"Yes," she said, "it's beautiful."

She took off the lid. There was nothing in the box. Woodgrain. Woodsmell. She started to cry. She covered her eyes and tried to stop.

"You'd best take that if you like it," Lyle said. He waited, hoping she would stop. He said firmly, "Jorie." She looked at him. His eyes were looking straight out of good weather.

"What?"

"It's no big deal, you know."

Nowadays the meadow isn't considered worth haying. Machinery is cost-prohibitive in relation to annual yield. No one will winter here anymore. We are a different breed of Westerners. Snow always looks good to skiers.

Someone from Denver bought Lyle's place for the fishing, a summer retreat. Without irrigation much of the meadow has regressed to native sidehill pasture and sage. The rest is frumpy-looking, matted under the yellow thatch of last year's uncut growth. Along the east fence, where Pat and Lyle used to bet on whether or not the snowdrift would last till the Fourth of July, short lengths of snowbroken wire sink into the earth, sink down with the roots.

Underneath its feral pelt, the meadow is still the meadow, entire, lying in wait for winter. Wildflowers still joy in its swells and hollows. And do the ruined, sage-choked irrigation ditches feel sorry for their intricately patterned uselessness?

Between the sky and the egg-shaped, egg-smooth granite boulder that floats out in the middle of the meadow's widest field, everything has its own green: cattails, willow leaves, the flip side of an aspen leaf, the gray-green sage, the yellow-green native pasture, the loden timber, all circling around, with that boulder at the center, as if the meadow were a green ear held up to listen to the sky's blue, and there is an axis drawn between the boulder and the sun.

Elsewhere on the mountain, most of the green stays locked in pines, the prairie is scorched yellow. But Lyle's meadow is a hemorrhage of green, and a green clockwork of waterways and grasses, held up to the sky in its ring of ridges, held up for the sky to listen, too.

The granite boulder is only there to hold it down.

A log cabin with a ruined roof sailed into the reservoir one morning, floating right down the middle, sure as a Viking ship with sinister purpose. It stopped over the deepest water behind the dam, becalmed. We all climbed up on the dam to look at it. Ray didn't know where it had come from, what crumbling bank delivered it to the spring-swollen creek, where it could have stood that he never saw it. Lyle didn't say anything.

It was made from a few oversized logs, suggesting deep snow country, at least a couple of miles away. Maybe the cabin had worked its way down for years from a high-country perch, riding floods till it snagged on rocks, and receding waters left it aground on sunbaked stones, waiting for the next chance. Water was high that year and it finally caught the ride it was waiting for.

Now it heeled over, pointing its open doorway at the sun.

Sometimes still, sometimes gently rolling over like a sleepy whale, the cabin lived a mysterious life for a couple of weeks at the center of the reservoir. One morning Ray woke to find it sidled up to shore in a small inlet, like it had had enough. He chained and locked it to a tree so it couldn't get away.

After the water went down the cabin lay grounded on its side, its door gaping—still chained to the tree.